Microsoft®
EXCEL 97

ENI Publishing LTD

500 Chiswick High Road
London W4 5RG

Tel : 0181 956 23 20
Fax : 0181 956 23 21

e-mail: publishing@ediENI.com
http://www.editions-eni.com

Editions ENI

BP 32125
44021 NANTES Cedex 1

Tel. 33.2.40.92.45.45
Fax 33.2.40.92.45.46

e-mail : editions@ediENI.com
http://www.editions-eni.com

Straight to the point collection directed by Corinne HERVO
Translated from the French by Gillian CAIN

Foreword

The aim of this book is to let you find rapidly how to perform any task in the spreadsheet **Excel 97**.

Each procedure is described in detail and illustrated so that you can put it into action easily.

The final pages are given over to an **index** of the topics covered and a set of **appendices**, which give details of shortcut keys, toolbars and integrated functions.

The typographic conventions used in this book are as follows:

Type faces used for specific purposes:

bold	indicates the option to take in a menu or dialog box.
italic	is used for notes and comments.
Ctrl	represents a key from the keyboard; when two keys appear side by side, they should be pressed simultaneously.

Symbols indicating the content of a paragraph:

▓	an action to carry out (activating an option, clicking with the mouse...).
⇨	a general comment on the command in question.
⌐🖑	a technique which involves the mouse.
⬡	a keyboard technique.
▤	a technique which uses options from the menus.

📖 OVERVIEW

📖 DOCUMENTS

📖 DATA

📖 CALCULATION

📖 PRESENTATION

1.1 The Excel environment

A-Starting/leaving Excel 97

▨ Click the **Start** button, move the mouse onto the **Programs** option and click **Microsoft Excel**.

▨ To leave,

| File | Click the 🗙 button | Alt F4 |
| Exit | in the application window | |

You may be prompted to save changes you have made in the documents which are open (the **Yes To All** option saves all open documents).

B-The workscreen

The Application window

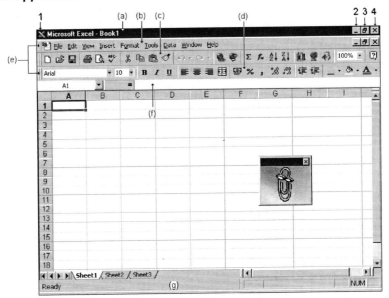

(a)	The title bar with the button for the **Control** menu (1), the **Minimize** (2), **Restore** (3) and **Close** (4) buttons.
(b)	The menu bar.
(c) (d)	The **Standard** and **Formatting** toolbars.
(e)	Move handles: to undock a toolbar or menu bar, double-click its move handle.
(f)	The formula bar.
(g)	The status bar.

The workbook window

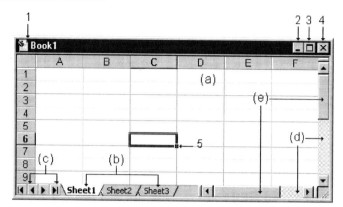

The workbook window contains the following items: the **Control** (1) menu button, the **Minimize** (2), **Maximize** (3) or **Restore** and **Close** (4) buttons.

(a)   The workspace: a worksheet is made up of **cells**; the black square at the bottom right-hand corner of the active cell is called the **fill handle** (5).

(b)   The worksheet tabs: open a sheet in the workbook by clicking its tab.

(c)   The tab scroll bar.

(d)   The scroll bars: drag the **scroll box** (e) or click the arrows to move up and down or across the active worksheet.

C-Dialog boxes

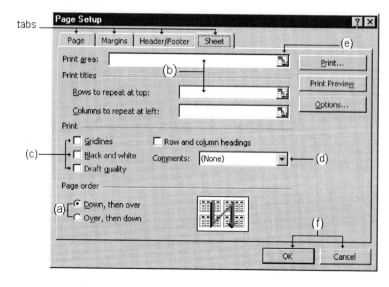

(a)   Option buttons: the active option is marked by a black dot.

(b)   Text boxes.

(c)   Check boxes: the box corresponding to the active object is checked.

(d)   List boxes: click the arrow to open and close the list (or press [Alt] [↓]).

(e)   The **Collapse dialog** button: click it to shrink the dialog box temporarily, leaving only the active text box on the screen. This allows you to select cells in the worksheet.

Click the [▦] button to display the dialog box at its normal size.

(f)   Command buttons: the **OK** button executes your command and closes the dialog box ([Enter] key); the **Cancel** button negates the command and closes the dialog box ([Esc] key).

▨ The keyboard keys [⇄] and [⇧ Shift] [⇄] can be used to access the various options. To go directly to an option, press [Alt] at the same time as the letter underlined in its name.

D-Shortcut menus

A shortcut menu is a limited menu containing options relevant to the selected item.

▨ To display the shortcut menu, select the item concerned then click the selection with the right mouse button.

▨ To remove the shortcut menu from the screen, press [Esc].

E-The Office Assistant

▨ Display the Office Assistant by clicking the [?] button.

▨ When you need help with the task you are working on, click the Office Assistant.

clic the topic
to see the help text

or enter a key word

start for the key word

to review tips already displayed

change the look of the assistant
and set other options

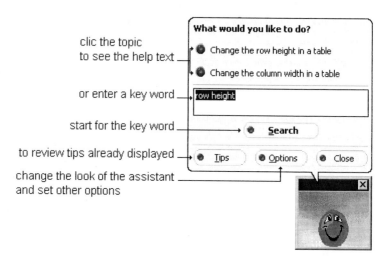

The Office Assistant displays a light bulb when it has some advice for you. Click the Assistant to see the advice.

To change the look of the assistant, right-click it then click **Choose Assistant**.

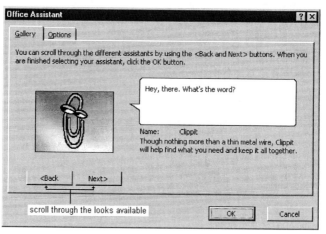

F- Repeating your last actions

If necessary select the item that you wish to repeat.

Edit
Repeat
 ⌷Ctrl⌷ **Y**

⇨ *If you have undone an action, click*  *to retrieve it.*

G-Undoing your last actions

▓ **Edit** Ctrl Z
Undo

▓ To undo several of your last actions, click the ⟲▾ button to open the list.

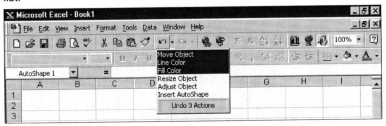

▓ Click the last action of the list you wish to undo (Excel undoes this action, and all those listed above it).

⟹ *Excel 97 allows you to cancel up to 16 of your last actions.*

H-Using help in Excel

▓ Click **Help** then **Contents and Index**.

▓ In the contents list or the index, find a reference to the topic which interests you.

▓ Double-click the reference for help with the topic.

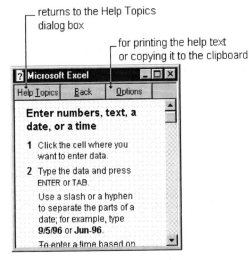

▓ Some dialog boxes have their own **Help** button. You can find out more about a particular option by clicking the [?] button then the option.

▓ For details of a window item, activate the **What's This ?** option in the **Help** menu, then click the item.

1.2 Managing what appears in the window

A-Freezing/unfreezing titles on the screen

▦ Click inside the column which follows the row titles you want to freeze, and/or click inside the row which comes after the column titles.

▦ **Window - Freeze Panes**

⇨ *To release the titles you have frozen use* **Window - Unfreeze Panes.**

B-Zooming in on the workspace

▦ **View - Zoom**

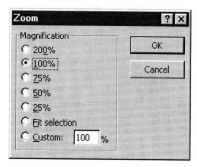

⇨ *The percentage of zoom can also be chosen from the list on the* **Standard** *toolbar.*

⇨ *To fit the worksheet to the size of the screen, use the command* **View - Full Screen.**

C-Hiding/displaying zero values

▦ **Tools - Options**
View tab

▦ Deactivate (or activate) the **Zero values** option.

⇨ *To hide zero values in selected cells only, apply a custom format (code 0;0;) to the cells.*

D-Displaying the results of a calculation

▦ Select the cells involved in the calculation.

▦ Right-click the status bar where **Sum** appears.

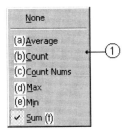

Six functions are proposed.

① Click the appropriate function:

(a) to display the average value of the selected cells.

(b) to display the number of alphanumerical or numerical values in the selection.

(c) to display the number of numerical values in the selection.

(d) to display the greatest value in the selection.

(e) to display the smallest value in the selection.

(f) to display the total of the values in the cells.

E-Displaying formulas instead of values

▨ **Tools - Options**
View tab

▨ Activate the **Formula** option under **Window**.

F-Unhiding/hiding an open workbook

▨ To display a hidden workbook: **Window - Unhide...** then double-click the file concerned.

▨ Use **Window - Hide** to hide the active workbook.

G-Docking/undocking a floating toolbar

▨ To dock a floating bar double-click the title bar.

▨ To undock a toolbar double-click its move handle: it becomes a floating toolbar.

H-Displaying/hiding a specific toolbar

░ Right-click any toolbar:

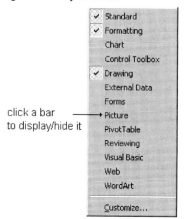

click a bar
to display/hide it

░ To display several toolbars, click **Customize** and select them in the list.

⇨ *Click* *to display or hide the Drawing toolbar.*

I- Creating a custom toolbar

░ **View - Toolbars - Customize**
░ Click the **New** button.
░ Give a name for the toolbar, then enter.
  A toolbar appears on the worksheet: it has no tools yet.
░ Add tools to the new bar.
░ When all the buttons have been added to the toolbar, click **Close**.

J- Managing tools in a toolbar on the screen

Deleting a tool

░ **View - Toolbars - Customize**
░ Drag the button to be deleted away from the bar and close the dialog box.

Adding a tool

░ **View - Toolbars - Customize**
░ Click the **Commands** tab.

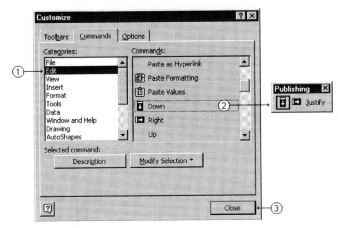

① Select the tool's category.

② Drag the tool button onto the bar.

③ Close the dialog box.

⇨ *Once a toolbar has been customised, you can retrieve the original version by clicking the **Restore** button in the **Customize** dialog box (**Toolbars** tab).*

1.3 Moving around/selecting in a worksheet

A-Moving around in a sheet

Use the scroll bars:

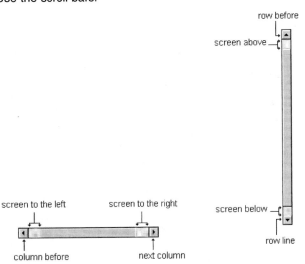

⇨ *As you drag the scroll box, Excel displays the row number or the column letter in a ScreenTip.*

Use the keyboard:

cell to the right/to the left	⟶ or ⇄/⟵ or ⬆Shift ⇄
cell above/below	⬆ or ⬆Shift Enter /⬇ or Enter
screen to the right/to the left	Alt Pg Dn /Alt Pg Up
screen above/below	Pg Up /Pg Dn
column A in the active row	Home
cell A1	Ctrl Home

⇨ *To reach a specific cell, select the reference of the active cell on the formula bar and enter the reference of the cell where you want to go.*

B-Finding a cell by its contents

If you want to search the whole sheet, activate cell A1, otherwise select the range concerned.

Edit - Find or Ctrl F

Enter the value which you want to find then indicate how to carry out the search.

C-Moving from one sheet to another

Using the tab scroll buttons, display the name of the sheet where you want to go. Click the tab to activate the sheet.

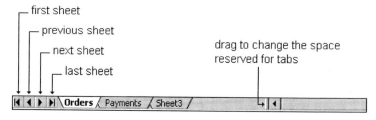

first sheet
previous sheet
next sheet
drag to change the space reserved for tabs
last sheet

⇨ *To scroll the tabs quickly, keep the* ⬆Shift *key pressed down while clicking* ◀ *or* ▶.

⇨ *On the keyboard you can use* Ctrl *to move to the next sheet or* Ctrl Pg Up *for the previous sheet.*

⇨ *To change the position of a sheet in the workbook, drag its tab.*

D-Selecting a range of adjoining cells

This can be done in three ways:

Dragging	Click the first cell of the selection and drag over the others. When you are satisfied with the selection, release the mouse button.
Click and ⬚ Shift	Click the first cell to be selected and then point the last one. Hold down ⬚ Shift then click at the same time. Release the mouse button before the ⬚ Shift key.
On the keyboard	Hold down the ⬚ Shift key and use the direction keys.

E-Selecting nonadjacent cells

Select the first cell/range of cells.

Point the first cell of the next range then press the Ctrl key and drag, if necessary, to select a range of cells.

Release the Ctrl key.

⇨ *In a formula or a dialog box, selected ranges which are nonadjacent are separated by a comma. For example: A5:A10,L5:L10 refers to the ranges of A5 to A10 and L5 to L10.*

F-Selecting rows and columns

The following methods can be used:

	Row	Column
🖱	Click the row number	Click the column letter
🎲	Activate a cell in the row and press ⬚ Shift space	Activate a cell in the column and press Ctrl space

⇨ *To select several rows (or columns) at a time, you can drag over them, or hold down ⬚ Shift and click.*

⇨ *To select the entire worksheet, click the button in the top left corner, where the column containing row numbers meets the row containing column letters or press Ctrl ⬚ Shift space .*

G-Selecting cells according to content

▨ Edit - Go To (or $\boxed{\text{F5}}$ or $\boxed{\text{Ctrl}}$ T)

▨ Click the **Special** button.

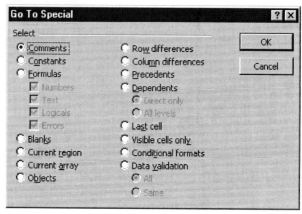

▨ Indicate the type of cells to be selected.

H-Tracing cells used in formulas

▨ Activate the cell containing the formula.

▨ **Tools - Auditing - Trace Precedents**

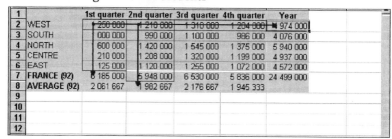

The precedent cells are surrounded with a border and linked to the calculation formula by an arrow.

⇨ *To delete the tracer arrows choose the option **Tools - Auditing - Remove All Arrows.***

2.1 Managing documents

A-Opening documents

▓ **File**
Open

[Ctrl] O

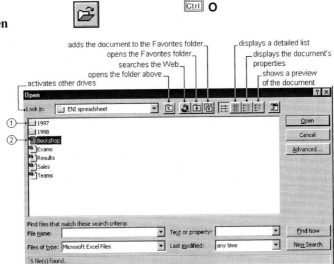

adds the document to the Favorites folder
opens the Favorites folder
searches the Web
opens the folder above
activates other drives

displays a detailed list
displays the document's properties
shows a preview of the document

① Open the folder containing the document by double-clicking its icon.

② To open a document, double-click its icon.

⇨ *You can open several documents at once: use the* [Ctrl] *and* [⇧ Shift] *keys to select them first.*

⇨ *The names of the last four documents appear at the end of the* **File** *menu: click one of them to open the document.*

⇨ *If you are working in a network, click* **Network Neighborhood** *in the* **Look in** *list to see all the workstations accessible.*

B-Activating an open document which is hidden

▓ **Window**

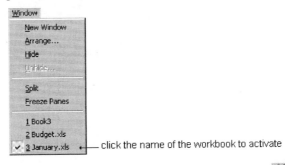

click the name of the workbook to activate

C-Saving a document

A new document

File
Save

   Ctrl S

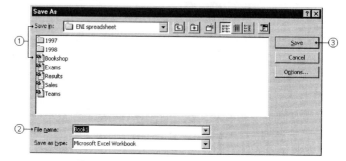

① Activate the disk and the folder where the document is to be saved.
② Give the document's name (up to 255 characters, including spaces).
③ Save the document.

⇨ *Excel documents have the extension .XLS (this may be hidden).*

Existing documents

File
Save

Ctrl S

⇨ *To update the summary of a document, use **File - Properties** and fill in the **Summary** tab.*

D-Choosing the default file location

Tools - Options
General tab

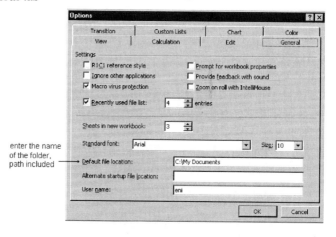

enter the name
of the folder,
path included

E-Activating document AutoSave

▨ Tools - AutoSave

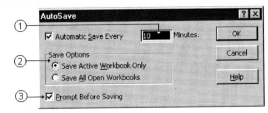

① Choose to run the AutoSave every five minutes, every ten minutes...

② Indicate which workbook to save.

③ Should Excel ask for confirmation before saving?

⇨ *The AutoSave option only appears in the Tools menu if the AutoSave add-in is installed (Tools - Add-ins).*

F-Closing documents

▨ **File**   Click in the   Ctrl F4 or Ctrl W
   Close   workbook window

▨ Save the document, if appropriate.

⇨ *To close all open documents, hold down the 󰀀 Shift key as you open the File menu then click Close All.*

G-Creating a new document

▨ **File**   ⬚   Ctrl N
   New
   OK

H-Protecting documents

▨ **File - Save As**

▨ Click **Options**.

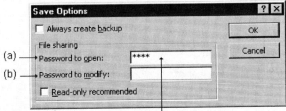

the password cannot be read

▨ Give the password required to access the document (a) or the password required to save modifications to the document (b).

DOCUMENTS

■ Type in the password again, to confirm it, and enter.

⇨ *Excel distinguishes between upper and lower-case letters in a password.*

I- Finding documents

■ In the **Open** dialog box:

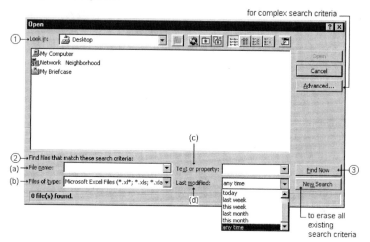

① Activate the drive or folder where you wish to search.

② Define the criteria of your search:

(a)   to search for a document by its name (you can use wildcard characters like * and ?).

(b)   to search for a specific type of document.

(c)   to indicate a string of characters in the document concerned, or one of its properties.

(d)   to search for a file by its date.

③ Start the search.

⇨ *To search the subfolders of the current folder or drive, click* 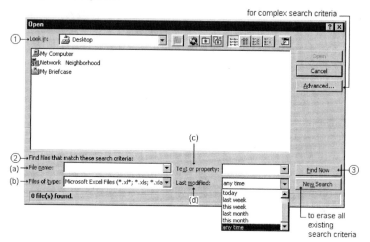 *and activate the option **Search Subfolders**.*

J- Sharing a workbook with other users

■ **Tools - Share Workbook**

■ Activate **Allow changes by more than one user at the same time.**

■ Click **OK** and save the workbook as usual.

Shared appears after the name of the workbook on the title bar.

Using a shared workbook

■ Open the workbook: you can add data, insert rows and columns, change the sort order, but you cannot delete worksheets or define conditional formats.

To see who else is using the workbook, open the **Tools - Share Workbook** dialog box: the list of current users appears on the **Editing** tab.

K-Establishing a hyperlink with another document

Select the cell in which you want the link to appear.

Insert
Hyperlink

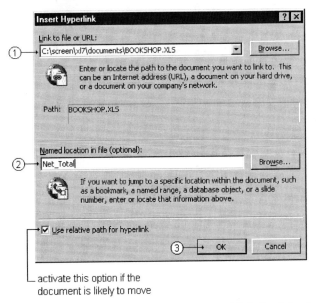

activate this option if the
document is likely to move

① Select the document with which you want to establish the link : it might be a document on one of your computer's disks, or on your network or at an Internet address.

② Specify the named range, bookmark, slide number... where you want the insertion point to be when the document opens.

③ Create the link.

		Quantity	Average Price
2			
3			
4		Quantity	Average Price
5	Novels	100	12,5
6	Comic Strips	719	6,2
7	Anthologies	180	11,0
8	S.F.	193	8,5
9	Biographies	104	20,1
10	Travel		26,5
11	Total		
12			
13	BOOKSHOP.XLS - Net_Total		
14			

a click on the hyperlink
opens the document

⇨ *To delete the link, clear the contents of the cell.*

2.2 Managing worksheets

A-Creating a link between worksheets

▒ Select the destination cells, type = and select the source cells.

▒ Validate by pressing [Ctrl] [⇧ Shift] [Enter].

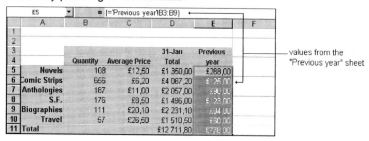

values from the "Previous year" sheet

⇨ *You could also use the command* Edit - Paste Special - Paste Link.

B-Copying/moving a sheet from one workbook to another

▒ Open the book from which you want to copy or move, and also the destination workbook.

▒ Activate the sheet then use **Edit - Move or Copy Sheet**.

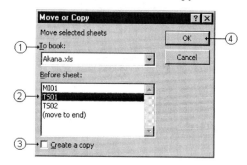

① Select the destination workbook.
② Select the existing sheet in front of which you want to insert.
③ Activate this option if you are making a copy.
④ Insert the sheet.

C-Deleting worksheets

▒ Select the worksheets to be deleted by holding down [Ctrl] and clicking their tabs then use **Edit - Delete Sheet**.

▒ Click **OK** to confirm.

D-Naming a worksheet

▓ Double-click the tab of the sheet you are going to name then type the new name over the former one (you are limited to 31 characters).

E-Working on several sheets at once

▓ Select all the sheets concerned by holding down the ⌨Ctrl key and clicking their tabs (this creates a workgroup). Do the typing, formatting... which will be applied to all the sheets in the group.

▓ To ungroup the sheets, click a tab which is not part of the group.

F-Protecting worksheets

▓ **Tools - Protect - Protect Workbook**

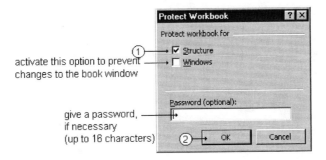

activate this option to prevent changes to the book window

give a password, if necessary (up to 16 characters)

① Check that the **Structure** option is active.

② Click **OK**.

▓ If you are setting a password, enter it a second time.

⇨ *To remove the protection from the workbook, use the command* **Tools - Protection - Unprotect Workbook**.

3.1 Entering data

A-Entering constants (text, values)

▨ Activate the cell where you want the data to appear then type the data.

cancels the data entry

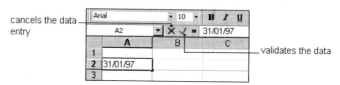

validates the data

▨ Activate the next cell you want to fill in.

⇨ *To enter several lines of data in a cell, press* Alt Enter *at the end of each line.*

⇨ *To enter the same data in several cells, select all the cells concerned, type the data (a formula, perhaps) and press* Ctrl Enter *to enter.*

⇨ *You can type in up 32000 characters in each cell. If you enter £10000, Excel will apply the format £10 000 immediately. To enter a percentage, type a % sign just after the number.*

⇨ *If you deactivate the option* **Move Selection after Enter** *accessible via* **Tools - Options - Edit** *tab, this prevents* Enter *from activating the next cell.*

B-AutoComplete: entering data semi-automatically

▨ Type in the first characters: Excel proposes an existing entry which begins with the same characters. To accept, press Enter .

▨ You can also see the list of existing entries in the column by pressing Alt Enter .

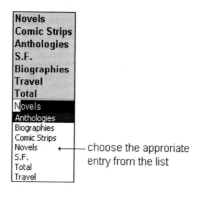

choose the approriate entry from the list

⇨ *The option* **Pick from List** *in the shortcut menu displays the same list.*

⇨ *This function only operates if the **Enable AutoComplete for cell values** option is active in the **Options** dialog box (**Tools - Options - Edit** tab).*

C-Inserting the PC's control date into a cell

▨ Activate the cell where you want to display the date.

▨ There are three ways to insert the computer's control date :

=TODAY()	The control date, updated each time the sheet is opened.
=NOW()	The control date and time, updated when the sheet is opened.
Ctrl ;	The control date, not changed automatically.

▨ Enter.

D-Entering data more quickly

▨ Select the cells that you want to fill in.

▨ When typing in a row of data press ⬅⬆ after each cell to move to the next. When typing in a column of data press Enter after each cell. If you need to return to the previous cell press ⇧ Shift ⬅⬆ or ⇧ Shift Enter .

E-Creating a data series

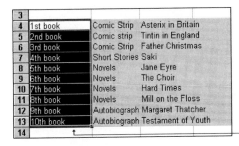

a data series is a logical progression

▨ Enter the first value of the series.

▨ Drag the fill handle from the active cell to the cell where you want to show the last value in the series.

⇨ *Select the first two values in a series for Excel to understand how it progresses: for example, January and March were selected to create this series.*

data series

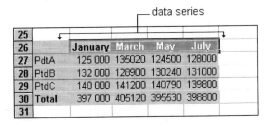

Microsoft Excel 97

F-Creating a custom data series

▨ Tools - Options
   Custom Lists tab

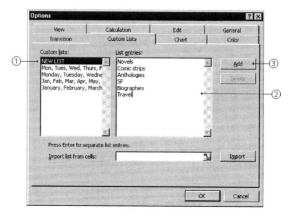

① Click **New list**.
② Enter the data, pressing ⌊⇧ Shift⌋ ⌊Enter⌋ to separate each entry.
③ Create the list.

G-Checking the spelling in a text

▨ If you only need to check part of the text, select it.

▨ Tools   ⌊F7⌋
   Spelling

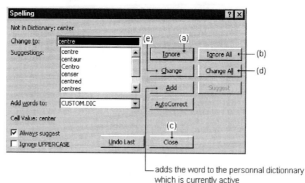

└─ adds the word to the personnal dictionnary
   which is currently active

▨ If the word is correctly spelt, click :

(a)   to leave the word unchanged and continue the check.

(b)   to leave a particular word unchanged each time it occurs.

(c)   to stop checking the spelling.

▨ If the word contains a mistake, correct it by a double-click on one of the suggestions or enter the correct spelling then click (d) or (e).

Click **OK** at the end of the spelling check.

⇨ *To delete a word which has accidentally been typed twice, click **Delete**.*

3.2 Editing data

A-Modifying cell contents

Double-click the cell concerned:

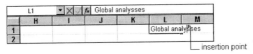

— insertion point

Make the changes (the ⌊Ins⌋ key switches between Insert mode and Over-type mode) then enter.

⇨ *You can also click the cell then edit its contents directly in the formula bar.*

B-Clearing cell contents

Select the cells to be cleared.

Drag the fill handle backwards over the selected cells to clear their contents.

⇨ *This technique deletes the contents of the cells without affecting their format. The command **Edit** - **Clear** allows you to indicate exactly what should be cleared (**Formats**, **Contents**, **Notes**...).*

C-Replacing cell contents

Select the cells concerned then use **Edit** - **Replace** (or ⌊Ctrl⌋**H**).

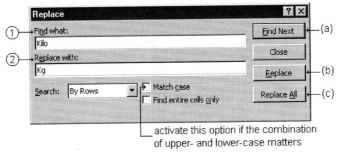

activate this option if the combination of upper- and lower-case matters

① Enter the text you wish to replace (this zone can contain wildcard characters: ? replaces one character; * replaces several).

② Enter the replacement text.

③ The replacements can be made individually (buttons (a) and (b)), or all at once (button (c)).

Microsoft Excel 97

DATA

3.3 Copying and moving data

A- Copying cell contents into adjacent cells

▓ Activate the cell you want to copy and point to its fill handle.

7 626FF	48 626FF
10 142FF	64 670FF
11 151FF	

▓ Drag the fill handle to the last destination cell.

B-Copying and moving cells

First method

▓ Select the source cells.

▓ Point the edge of the selected range.

▓ If you are copying, press the [Ctrl] key and, without releasing it, drag the cells to their destination.

If the cells are being moved, just drag them to their new position.

▓ Release the mouse button, then the [Ctrl] key, if you have been using it.

⇨ *To move a range of cells to another worksheet, hold down the* [Alt] *key as you drag the selected range onto the tab of the sheet concerned then to the first cell of the destination range. To copy cells to another worksheet, hold down both the* [Ctrl] *and* [Alt] *keys as you drag.*

Second method

▓ Select the source cells.

▓ If you are copying the cells, use:

Edit [Ctrl] C
Copy

▓ If you are moving the cells, use:

Edit [Ctrl] X
Cut

▓ Activate the first cell of the destination range.

▓ **Edit** [Ctrl] V
Paste

C-Transposing rows and columns while copying

▓ Select the data to be copied, go into **Edit - Copy** then activate the first destination cell.

▓ **Edit - Paste Special**

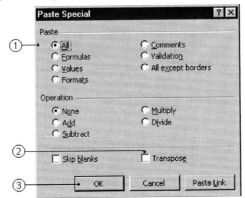

① Activate the option corresponding to what you are copying.

② Choose **Transpose**.

③ Click **OK**.

D-Sorting data in a table

▓ Select the table you want to sort.

▓ To sort by a single criterion, activate a cell in the column you want to sort by then click ⬚ to sort in ascending order or ⬚ to sort in descending order.

⇨ *To sort by several criteria, use the command Data - Sort.*

DATA

3.4 Named ranges

A-Naming cells

First method

▨ Select the range of cells which you want to name then use the command **Insert - Name - Define** (or ⌨Ctrl⌨F3).

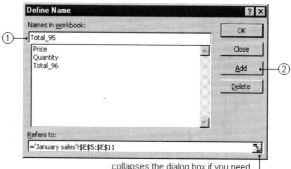

collapses the dialog box if you need ⌐
to modify the selection

① Enter the name for the range.

② Add the new name to the list.

▨ Go on to define any other names then click **OK**.

⇨ *There must be no spaces or hyphens in these names!*

⇨ *To name a calculation formula, enter the formula in the **Refers to** box. To use a formula with a name, type = followed by the name of the formula, and enter.*

Second method

This method is useful if the names that you want to apply to the cells are adjacent to them.

▨ Select the cells containing the names to be used and the cells that you want to name.

▨ **Insert - Name - Create** (or ⌨Ctrl⌨⇧Shift⌨F3)

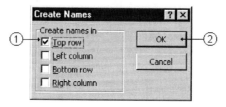

① Indicate the position of the cells containing the names.

② Click **OK**.

B-Using a name in a formula

▒ While you are typing the formula, type the name instead of the cell references or paste the name into the formula using the command **Insert - Name - Paste** (or ⌧⌧).

C-Replacing cell references with their name

▒ Select the cells where you want to replace references by names.

▒ **Insert - Name - Apply**

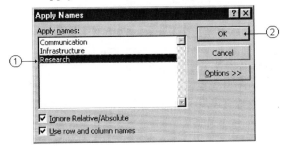

① Select the names concerned.

② Click **OK**.

4.1 Calculations

A-Entering a calculation formula

▦ Activate the cell which will display the result.

▦ Type = or click the = button on the formula bar.

▦ Activate the first cell involved in the calculation (click the cell or use the arrow keys to move the pointer).

▦ Indicate the mathematical operation to perform.

▦ Repeat for each of the cells involved in the calculation:

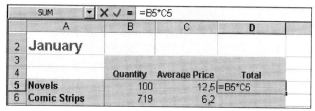

▦ When you reach the last cell, either click the ☑ button or press the Enter key.

⇨ *If you know the cell references you can type them in rather than using the mouse or arrow keys to point to them.*

⇨ *A click on the formula bar's = button displays the formula palette: using the palette makes it easier to insert a function into a formula.*

B-Adding up a group of cells

▦ Activate the cell which is going to display the result.

▦ Click Σ or press Alt =.

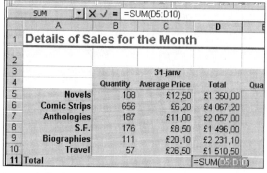

▦ If you are not satisfied with this selection, change it. Enter.

C-Including an absolute cell reference in a formula

An absolute cell reference does not evolve when the formula is copied.

▓ Start entering the formula, stopping after the cell reference that you want to make absolute. If you are editing an existing formula, position the insertion point after the cell reference.

▓ Press ⌊F4⌋.

the $ signs show that the row and column references are absolute

SUM	▼	X ✓ =	=D5*D13		
	A	B	C	D	E	F
3						
4		Quantity	Average Price	Cost Price	VAT	
5	Novels	£100,00	£12,50	£1 250,00	=D5*D13	
6	Comic Strips	£719,00	£6,20	£4 457,80		
7	Anthologies	£180,00	£11,00	£1 980,00		
8	S.F.	£193,00	£8,50	£1 640,50		
9	Biographies	£104,00	£20,10	£2 090,40		
10	Travel	£82,00	£26,50	£2 173,00		

▓ Complete the formula if necessary, then enter.

⇨ *Press* ⌊F4⌋ *again for only the row number to remain absolute, and again for the column number.*

D-Carrying out simple calculations while copying

While you are copying data, you can carry out a mathematical operation (adding, subtracting...) which combines the data being copied with the destination data.

▓ Select the data you wish to copy and go into **Edit - Copy**.

▓ Activate the first destination cell then use **Edit - Paste Special**.

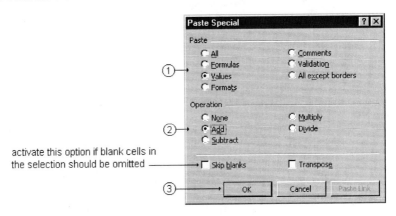

activate this option if blank cells in
the selection should be omitted

① Indicate what it is that you want to copy.
② Select the mathematical operation.
③ Make the copy.

CALCULATION

E-Adding statistics to a table by inserting subtotals

▨ Sort the table by the column containing the entries you want to group together, as a first step to producing a subtotal for each group.

▨ Select the table then use **Data - Subtotals**.

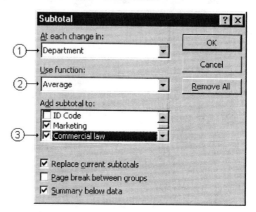

① Select the column used for grouping.

② Choose the type of statistic you require for each group.

③ Mark the columns containing the values involved in the calculation.

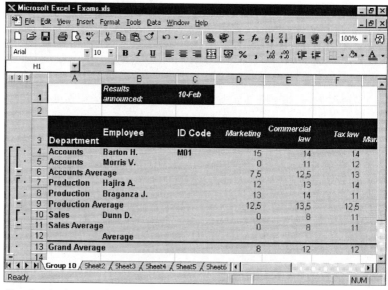

Excel calculates subtotals, which provide the statistics required, and creates an outline.

F- Consolidating worksheets

This enables you to carry out an analysis (for example, a sum) of values contained in several tables.

▦ Activate the first cell of the range where you wish to display the results.

▦ **Data - Consolidate**

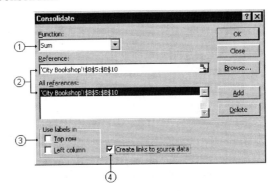

① Choose the calculation you want to perform.

② For each sheet involved in the consolidation: activate the sheet and select the cells concerned then click the **Add** button.

③ If you have included data labels in your selection, indicate where they are located.

④ If you wish to create a permanent link between the source sheets and the destination sheet, mark the check box.

G-Changing the calculation mode

▦ **Tools - Options**
Calculation tab

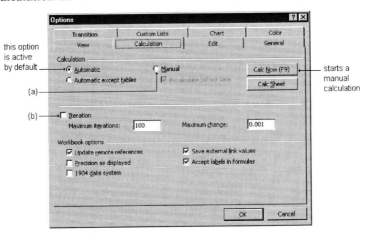

(a)   suspends automatic calculation.

(b)   enables calculation involving circular references.

H-Creating a two-input data table

this cell contains the formula

number of payments

	A	B	C	D	E	F
1	Capital	10000				
2	Interest rate	11%				
3	Payments	12				
4						
5	883,82	12	18	24	30	36
6	£10 000,00	£883,82	£605,19	£466,08	£382,78	£327,39
7	£20 000,00	£1 767,63	£1 210,37	£932,16	£765,56	£654,77
8	£30 000,00	£2 651,45	£1 815,56	£1 398,24	£1 148,34	£982,16
9	£40 000,00	£3 535,27	£2 420,74	£1 864,31	£1 531,12	£1 309,55
10	£50 000,00	£4 419,08	£3 025,93	£2 330,39	£1 913,90	£1 636,94
11	£60 000,00	£5 302,90	£3 631,11	£2 796,47	£2 296,68	£1 964,32
12	£70 000,00	£6 186,72	£4 236,30	£3 262,55	£2 679,46	£2 291,71
13	£80 000,00	£7 070,53	£4 841,48	£3 728,63	£3 062,25	£2 619,10
14	£90 000,00	£7 954,35	£5 446,67	£4 194,71	£3 445,03	£2 946,48
15	£100 000,00	£8 838,17	£6 051,85	£4 660,78	£3 827,81	£3 273,87

sum borrowed   results

This table shows how the amount paid back monthly on a loan varies according to the number of instalments and the sum borrowed.

In two cells located outside the table, enter initial input values for the calculation.

Enter the variable data - one series in a row, and the other series in a column.

At the intersection of the row and the column enter the calculation formula, referring to the input cells outside the table.

Select the range of cells including the formula and all the result cells.

Data - Table

In the **Row Input Cell** box indicate which of the two input cells referred to in the formula corresponds to the variable data in the row.

Indicate which is the **Column Input Cell**.

Enter.

4.2 Complex calculations

A-Calculating with array formulas

Proceed as for an ordinary calculation but work with cell ranges instead of individual cells and enter with [Ctrl] [⇧ Shift] [Enter] , not [Enter] or [Ctrl] [Enter] .

B12	▼	= {=(B2:D5-$E2:$E5)/$E2:$E5}							
	A	B	C	D	E	F	G	H	I
1		BRISTOL	BATH	TAUNTON	Average				
2	Accountant	99.75	98.5	98.6	98.95				
3	Secretary	72	73.55	71.9	72.48				
4	Shop Manager	92	94.8	93.83	93.54				
5	Truck-driver	70.35	73.32	69.8	71.16				
6									
7									
8	% difference in relation to the regional average								
9									
10									
11		BRISTOL	BATH	TAUNTON					
12	Accountant	0.81%	-0.45%	-0.35%					
13	Secretary	-0.67%	1.47%	-0.80%					
14	Shop Manager	-1.65%	1.34%	0.31%					
15	Truck-driver	-1.13%	3.04%	-1.91%					

You can recognise an array formula by the braces surrounding it.

⇨ *Using an array formula instead of several formulas takes up less memory. Certain functions can only be applied to arrays.*

B-Calculations involving several unknown quantities

Example of a problem: find the quantity of factors x, y and z required to produce quantities q1, q2 and q3.

Enter in the form of an array all the elements of the linear analysis as well as the results you are aiming for.

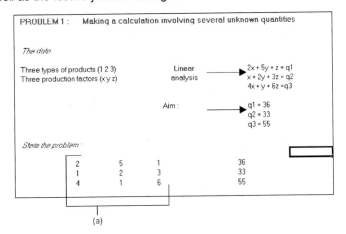

PROBLEM 1 : Making a calculation involving several unknown quantities

The data

Three types of products (1 2 3)
Three production factors (x y z)

Linear
analysis
→ 2x + 5y + z = q1
x + 2y + 3z = q2
4x + y + 6z = q3

Aim :
→ q1 = 36
q2 = 33
q3 = 55

State the problem :

2	5	1		36
1	2	3		33
4	1	6		55

(a)

- Calculate the inverse matrix (a): select the cells on your worksheet which will contain the array of the inverse matrix then use the =MINVERSE(array) function and validate with ⌈Ctrl⌉ ⌈⇧ Shift⌉ ⌈Enter⌉ .
- Calculate the product of the two arrays: select the destination cells for the result then use the function =MMULT(array1, array2) (where array1 contains as many columns as array2 has rows) and press ⌈Ctrl⌉ ⌈⇧ Shift⌉ ⌈Enter⌉ to enter.

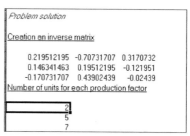

In this example, to produce 36 of product 1, 33 of product 2, and 55 of product 3, you will need 2 units of factor x, 5 of factor y and 7 of factor z.

C-Setting a goal value

- Activate the cell you wish to set to a certain value and ensure that it contains a calculation formula.
- **Tools - Goal Seek**
- Set the goal value in the **To value** box and indicate which is the cell containing the variable value in **By changing cell**. Enter.

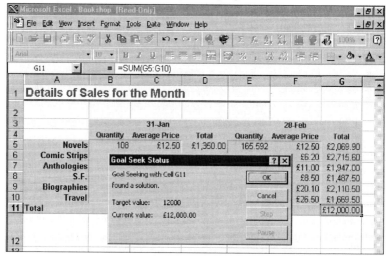

- To accept the result suggested by Excel, click **OK**. To return to the original values, click **Cancel**.

D-Solving problems with Solver

▨ **Tools - Solver**

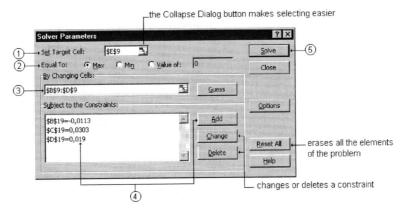

the Collapse Dialog button makes selecting easier

erases all the elements of the problem

changes or deletes a constraint

① Give the reference of the target cell.

② Indicate whether the cell is to be maximised, minimised or set to a specific value.

③ Click this box then select the changing (variable) cells in the worksheet.

④ Enter the constraints one at a time: click **Add**, activate the cell concerned and specify the constraint.

⑤ Start the solving process.

▨ If the result is satisfactory, keep the solution by clicking **Keep Solver Solution**, otherwise choose the **Restore Original Values** option. Click **OK** (you could also click **Save Scenario** to save the solutions which Solver finds).

⇨ *Click the* **Options** *button in the* **Solver Parameters** *dialog box to access the options* **Save Model** *and* **Load Model**. *These are used for saving all the elements of a problem and retrieving them later.*

4.3 Functions

A-Inserting a function into a formula

Excel 97's formula palette makes this much easier.

▨ Click the = button to display the formula palette.

▨ Select the function from the first list in the formula palette. If the function you need does not appear in the list, click **More functions**.

⬛ Define each of the function's arguments, for example:

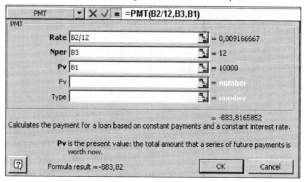

⬛ If necessary, finish the formula, then click **OK**.

⮕ *Pressing* ⬚Shift⬚ ⬚F3⬚ *opens the Paste function dialog box, where you can select a function from one of several categories.*

B-Calculating simple statistics

⬛ Use one of the following common functions:

=AVERAGE()	to calculate the average value of a set of cells.
=MAX()	to extract the maximum value.
=MIN()	to extract the minimum value.

C-Setting a condition

⬛ Enter your condition, taking care to follow the syntax:
=IF(condition,action if TRUE,action if FALSE)

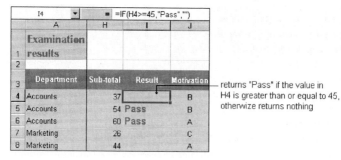

returns "Pass" if the value in H4 is greater than or equal to 45, otherwize returns nothing

⬛ A variety of actions can be performed in a conditional expression:

Display a number	enter the number
Display a text	enter the text between quotation marks
Display the result of a calculation	enter the calculation formula

36

Display the contents of a cell	point to the cell
Display a zero	enter nothing
No display	type ""

⇨ *You can set multiple conditions, linking them with the operators AND and/or OR.*

I8	▼	**=** =IF(OR((H8>45),(AND(H8>=40,J8="A"))),"Pass","")

	A	H	I	J	K	L
	Examination					
1	**results**					
2						
3	**Department**	**Sub-total**	**Result**	**Motivation**		
4	Accounts	37		B		this candidate passes
5	Accounts	54	Pass	B		because H4 is greater than 40
6	Accounts	60	Pass	A		and the "Motivation"
7	Marketing	26		C		value is A
8	Marketing	44	Pass	A		
9	Marketing	46	Pass	B		

D-Managing lookup tables

In this example, when the code of a book is entered, the function returns the title and author.

Item Code	Category	Title	Author	Price
CI011	Classics	The Woman...	Collins W.	£ 4.50
CI108	Classics	Confessions...	De Quincey T.	£ 4.99
CI401	Classics	Persuasion	Austin J.	£ 4.50
Co150	Contemporary	London Fields	Amis M.	£ 6.79
Co203	Contemporary	Brownout	MO T.	£ 6.79
Hi300	History	Richelieu	Fraser A.	£ 3.99

| ◄ | ►| ►I| \Sheet1 / Sheet2 / Sheet3 / Sheet4 / Sheet5 / Sheet6 / | ◄ | ► |

H13	▼	=IF(G13<>"",LOOKUP(G13,Item_Code,Title&" "&Author),"")

	E	F	G	H	I
11					
12			Item Code	Category and Title	Price
13			CI108	Confessions... De Quincey T.	4.99
14			Co150	London Fields Amis M.	6.79
15			Co203	Brownout MO T.	6.79
16			Hi300	Richelieu Fraser A.	3.99
17					
18					

▨ A lookup table is made up of a row (or column) containing a list of "compare values", and other rows (or columns), which list associated information. The table should be sorted in ascending order of the compare values.

▨ In the cell where the information is to be displayed, use the following function:
LOOKUP(lookup_value,lookup_vector,result_vector)

Microsoft Excel 97

CALCULATION

lookup_value	is the compare value, a value which can be entered in a cell or directly into the formula.
lookup_vector	is the search range for the compare value.
result_vector	is the search range for the corresponding data.

E-Making scenarios

A scenario enables you to solve a problem by considering several hypotheses.

Creating scenarios

▪ Tools - Scenarios
▪ Click **Add**.

① Enter a name for the scenario.

② Delete whatever appears in the **Changing Cells** box.

Click ▦ and hold down ⌨Ctrl while selecting from the sheet the data which changes in this scenario. Click ▦ to restore the dialog box.

③ Click **OK** then enter the values for each changing cell and click **OK**.

▪ Create any other scenarios in the same way.

Running a scenario

▓ **Tools - Scenario Manager**

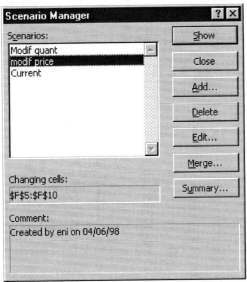

▓ If you only want to run one scenario select it then click **Show**. The result will be shown on your worksheet. If you want to run all the scenarios, click **Summary**.

▓ If you wish, select the cells which interest you.

▓ Enter.

The summary is presented as an outline on a separate worksheet.

CALCULATION

5.1 Rows and columns

A-Inserting rows and columns

- Select the row/column before the position where you are going to insert the new row(s)/column(s).
- Point to the fill handle. Hold down the ⇧ Shift key as you drag the fill handle over as many rows/columns as you wish to insert.
- Release the mouse button first, then the ⇧ Shift key.

⇨ *If you need to insert new rows above line 1, or columns before column A, use the command Insert - Rows or Columns.*

B-Deleting rows and columns

- Select the rows (or columns) to be deleted.
- Point to the fill handle and hold down the ⇧ Shift key as you drag upwards for rows (to the left for columns) over the rows (or columns) to be deleted.
- Release the mouse button, then the ⇧ Shift key.

C-Modifying the width of a column/height of a row

- Select each column to be resized to the same width (or each row to be given the same new height); if only one column or row is concerned, do not select it.
- Point to the vertical line on the right of one of the selected columns (or to the horizontal line under one of the row numbers)
- Drag to the size required.

D-Adjusting the height of a row automatically

- Activate a cell which is not tall enough to display all the text it contains.
- **Format - Cell** (or Ctrl1)
  Alignment tab
- Activate the **Wrap Text** option.

⇨ *You can adjust column widths to fit the longest value in the column, and row heights to the tallest value in the row. For column width, double-click the vertical line to the right of the column letter. For row height, double-click the horizontal line below the row number.*

E-Applying an automatic format to a table

▓ Select the table to be formatted then use **Format - AutoFormat**.

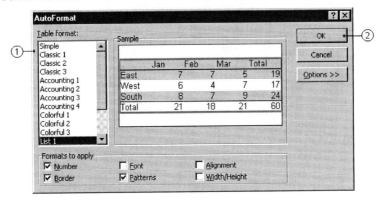

① Choose the format.
② Apply the format.

⇨ *To customise an AutoFormat, click the **Options** button to deactivate the attributes you do not want.*

5.2 Cells

A-Inserting blank cells

▓ Select the cell before the position where you are going to insert the new cell(s).

▓ Hold down the ⌈⇧ Shift⌉ key and drag the fill handle downwards (or to the right) over as many cells as you wish to insert.

⇨ *To move cells and insert them between existing cells elsewhere in the sheet, select them and point to one edge of the selected range. Holding the ⌈⇧ Shift⌉ key down, drag the cells into position.*

B-Deleting cells

▓ Select the cells to be deleted.

▓ Drag the fill handle upwards while keeping the ⌈⇧ Shift⌉ key pressed down.

⇨ *The gap left by the deleted cells is filled by moving up the cells below. If you prefer to move the cells from right to left, use **Edit - Delete**.*

PRESENTATION

C-Limiting the cells where data can be entered

If you want to authorise writing in certain cells only, you should first un-lock these cells, then apply protection to the whole sheet.

Unlocking selected cells

- Select the cells where writing is allowed then use **Format - Cells** (or [Ctrl]**1**).
- Deactivate **Locked** under the **Protection** tab.

Protecting the sheet

- **Tools - Protection - Protect Sheet**

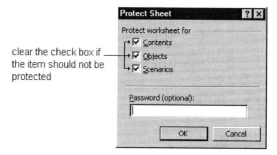

clear the check box if the item should not be protected

- Enter a password if you require one, otherwise press [Enter].
- Enter the password a second time to confirm.
- ⇨ *On protected sheets, certain formatting options become unavailable.*
- ⇨ *To remove the protection from a sheet, use the command **Tools - Protection - Unprotect Sheet**. If necessary give the password which protects the sheet, then enter.*

D-Attaching comments to cells

- Activate the cell with which you want to associate a comment then use **Insert - Comment** (or [⇧ Shift] [F2]).
- Enter the text of the comment (use [Enter] to change lines).

- To read the comment, point the cell: a red triangle marks the top right corner of a cell with a comment.
- ⇨ *Use the buttons on the **Revision** bar to manage comments.*

5.3 Formatting

A-Formatting numerical values

▦ Select the values concerned and choose one of the following three formats:

	Currency	(£10 000)
	Percent	(100 000%)
	Comma	(10,000)

⇨ *If number symbols (#) appear in certain cells, widen the column.*

⇨ *To show more, or fewer decimal places, select the cells concerned and use the* ⊞ *or* ⊞ *tool buttons. Additional formats are available in the* **Format - Cells** *dialog box.*

B-Formatting dates

▦ Select the dates to be formatted then use **Format - Cells** (or ⌨1).

▦ If necessary activate the **Number** tab.

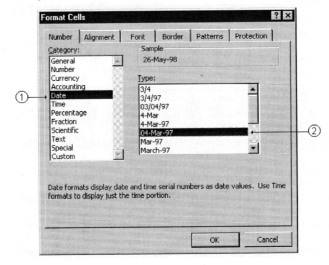

① Choose the category **Date**.
② Select the format.

C-Creating a custom format

▓ Select the cells to which you want to apply the format.

▓ **Format - Cells** (or ⌨1)
Number tab

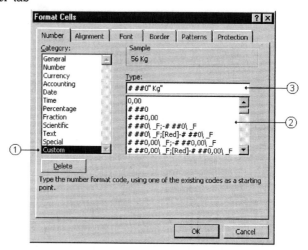

① Select the **Custom** category.

② Choose the format closest to what you have in mind.

③ Enter your custom format.

⇨ *When text is being added to a format, it must be entered between quotation marks.*

⇨ *For hiding cell contents, create a format ;;; (three semi-colons).*

D-Creating conditional formats

▓ Select the cells concerned.

▓ **Format - Conditional Formatting**

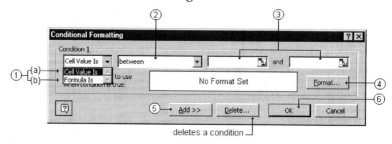

deletes a condition ⌐

① Choose:

    (a)   if the condition applies to a value contained in the selected cells

    (b)   if the condition applies to a formula.

② If you have chosen (a), select an operator of comparison. If you have chosen (b), give the formula.
③ If necessary, set further conditions.
④ Define the format which will be applied to the cells if the condition is met then click the **Format - Cells** dialog box's **OK** button.
⑤ Define additional formats if you need to.
⑥ Create the format(s).

E-Modifying the orientation of a text

▨ Select the cells concerned.
▨ **Format - Cells** (or [Ctrl] 1)
▨ Under the **Alignment** tab choose **Orientation**:

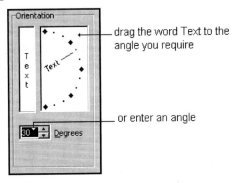

drag the word Text to the angle you require

or enter an angle

F-Aligning cell contents

▨ Select the cells concerned then click ▤ left alignment, ▤ centered or ▤ right alignment.

▨ **Format - Cells** (or [Ctrl] 1)
Alignment tab

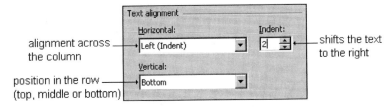

alignment across the column

position in the row (top, middle or bottom)

shifts the text to the right

Microsoft Excel 97

⇨ *To centre cell contents across several columns, select the cells across which the text should be centred (the first cell in the range must contain the text) and click* ▣.

G-Modifying the font and/or size of the characters

▦ Select the cells or characters concerned then choose the font, size and colour from the list boxes on the **Formatting** toolbar.

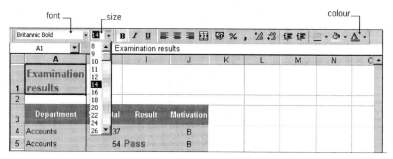

⇨ *To adjust the size of the characters automatically when there is not enough space in the cell to display the entire contents of a cell, use* **Format - Cells - Alignment** *tab and activate the* **Shrink to fit** *option.*

H-Formatting characters

Select the cells or characters concerned then activate the attribute(s) you want to apply:

B	[Ctrl] B	**bold**
I	[Ctrl] I	*italique*
U	[Ctrl] U	underlined

⇨ *If you repeat the same action for the same text, you cancel the corresponding attribute.*

Select the cells or characters concerned then use **Format - Cells** (or Ctrl 1) **Font** tab.

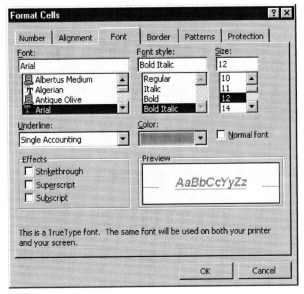

Activate all the formats to be applied to the text.

I- Drawing borders around cells

Select the cells concerned then choose a border from the palette on the **Formatting** toolbar.

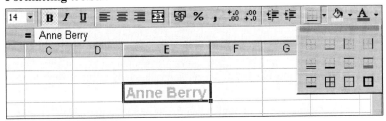

Select the cells concerned and use **Format - Cells** (or Ctrl 1), **Border** tab.

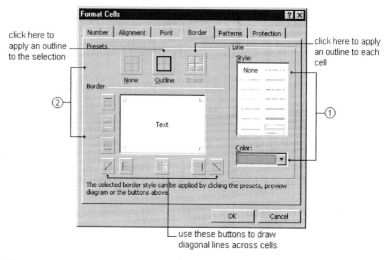

click here to apply an outline to the selection

click here to apply an outline to each cell

use these buttons to draw diagonal lines across cells

① Choose a style and a colour.

② Indicate the position of the lines making up the border.

J- Colouring/shading cells

Select the cells that you want to colour then open the [🖌️ ▾] list and choose a colour.

Select the cells that you want to colour or shade then use **Format - Cells** (or Ctrl 1), **Patterns** tab.

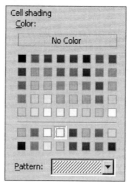

Choose a **Colour** and a **Pattern**.

K-Reproducing a format

▒ Select the cells whose formats you want to copy.

▒ Click 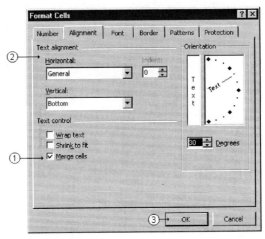.

▒ Select the cells to which you want to apply the format.

⇨ *To copy formats or the results of calculations, copy the data into the clipboard then use* **Edit - Paste Special.**

L-Merging cells

▒ Select the cells concerned (only the data in the first cell of the selection will appear in the merged cells).

▒ **Format - Cell** (or Ctrl **1**)
Alignment tab

① Activate this option.

② If necessary, specify the alignment that you wish to apply to the data.

③ Click **OK.**

5.4 Styles and templates

A-Creating a style

Save a collection of attributes as a style then apply them all at once as often as you need to.

▨ Activate the cell whose formatting is to be saved as a style.

▨ **Format - Style** (or ⌨Alt⌨ ')

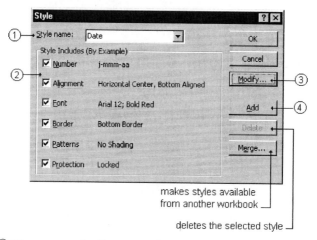

makes styles available
from another workbook ⏌

deletes the selected style ⏌

① Give a name for the new style.

② Deactivate any attributes you do not require.

③ If you need to, make changes to the formatting.

④ Create the style.

B-Using a style

▨ Select the cells to be formatted.

▨ **Format - Style** (or ⌨Alt⌨ ')

▨ Select the style and enter.

C-Creating a template

▨ To transform a worksheet into a template, delete from it everything which you do not need to reproduce in other documents, and activate any appropriate protections.

▨ **File - Save As**

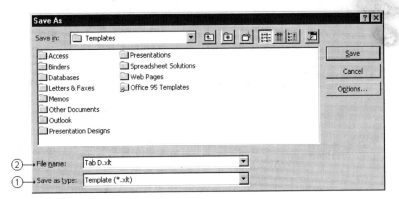

① Choose **Template**.

② Give the template a name.

⇨ *All templates have the extension XLT.*

D-Using a template

░ **File - New** (or Ctrl N)

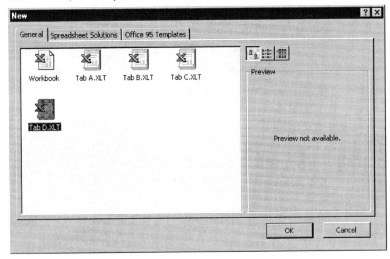

░ If the **Spreadsheet Solutions** page is not already open, click its tab then double-click the name of the template you wish to use. When you open a template, Excel copies its contents into a new worksheet.

░ Use the new workbook and save it as usual.

PRESENTATION

5.5 Outlines

A-Creating the outline of a table

When you are not interested in the details of a calculation, creating an outline allows you to view or print just the results.

Automatically

▦ Select the table concerned.

▦ **Data - Group and Outline - AutoOutline**

Manually

▦ Select the rows (or columns) that you do not need to see.

▦ Click ⬛ on the **Query and Pivot** toolbar.

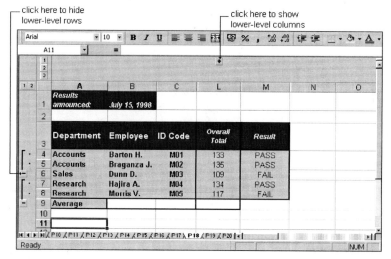

⇨ *To remove or add a row/column in the outline, select it, then click ⬛ or ⬛.*

B-Destroying an outline

▦ Select the table concerned.

▦ **Data - Group and Outline - Clear Outline**

6.1 Printing

A-Printing a sheet

Activate the sheet to be printed then click the 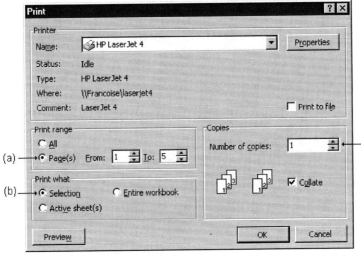 tool.

B-Printing part of a sheet

File - Print (Ctrl P) or click the Print button in Print Preview.

(a) prints a group of pages.

(b) prints a range which is currently selected.

C-Creating a print area

You can define the part of the sheet you want to print as a print area.

Select the range to be printed.

File - Print Area - Set Print Area

⇨ *Excel keeps the last print area created in memory.*

⇨ *To delete the print area use File - Print Area - Clear Print Area.*

D-Managing page breaks

░ Activate the cell which is going to be the first of your new page.

░ **Insert - Page Break**

	A	H	I	J·	K	L
1	Examination			the page break is represented		
2				by a dotted line		
3	Department	Sub-total	Result	Motivation		
4	Accounts	37		B		
5	Accounts	54	Pass	B		

⇨ *To delete the page break, activate a cell in the next row or column and use* **Insert - Remove Page Break***.*

⇨ *The command* **View - Page Break Preview** *makes the page breaks visible as blue lines on the worksheet. To move a page break, drag the blue line representing it.*

E-Repeating titles on each page

You can repeat rows and/or columns, often those containing titles, on each printed page.

░ **File - Page Setup**
Sheet tab

░ Activate the **Rows to Repeat at Top** box then select the rows and/or activate **Columns to Repeat at Left** and select the columns.

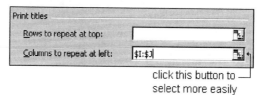

click this button to —⌐
select more easily

F- Previewing a printed sheet

Displaying the Print Preview

▓ **File**
Print Preview

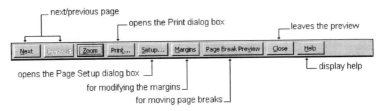

Print Preview buttons

▓ To zoom in on a preview, place the mouse pointer on the item to be magnified and click.

⇨ *Before you click, the mouse pointer appears as a magnifying glass; afterwards it becomes an arrow.*

⇨ *To return to the scaled-down preview, click the page again.*

▓ To change the width of margins and columns widths, click the **Margins** button.

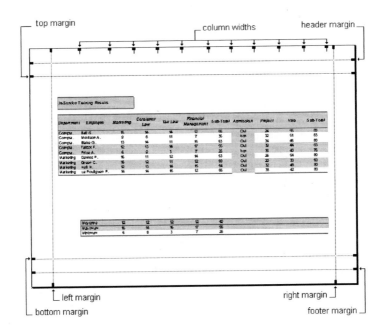

▓ Drag the appropriate handle.

6.2 Page setup

A-Modifying page setup options

▒ **File - Page Setup** or click the **Setup** button in the Print Preview.
▒ Activate the **Margins** tab.

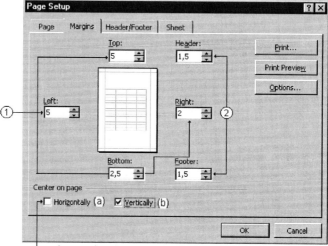

└─ activate or deactivate (a) and/or (b)
to indicate how to centre the table

① Set the margins for printing.
② Set the positions of the header and footer.

▒ Modify the **Scaling** options under the **Page** tab.

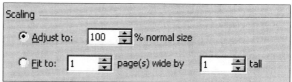

▒ Choose the appropriate **Orientation** under the **Page** tab.

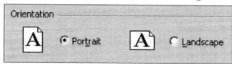

▒ To print a sheet without gridlines, deactivate **Gridlines** on the **Sheet** tab.

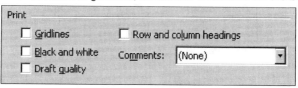

B-Creating headers and footers

▩ **File - Page Setup** or click the **Setup** button in the Print Preview. **Header/Footer** tab

You could also use the command **View - Header/Footer**.

▩ Click the **Custom Header** or **Custom Footer** button.

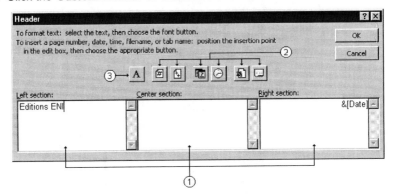

① Enter the text to be printed in the box which corresponds to the position on the page where you want the header/footer to appear. To create a second (third...) line of text, press Enter.

② To insert variable details click the appropriate buttons.

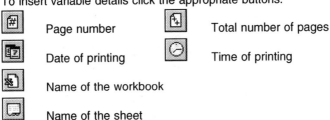

Page number   Total number of pages

Date of printing   Time of printing

Name of the workbook

Name of the sheet

③ Format the text.

➪ *Lists of popular headers and footers are also available under the* **Header/Footer** *tab (if you select a header/footer from the list, it is automatically centred on the page).*

6.3 Views and reports

A-Using views

In a view you save one of a set of possible print areas and page setup parameters. When you switch to a view these options are automatically activated.

Creating a view

▦ Prepare the sheet for printing (page setup, print area, hiding columns).

▦ **View - Custom Views - Add**

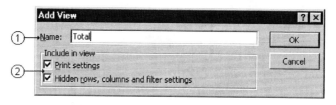

① Enter the name of the view being created.

② Indicate the elements which should be included in the view.

Using a view

▦ **View - Custom Views**

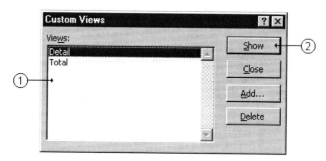

① Select the view.

② Activate the view.

B-Creating a report

A report prints a series of views in succession.

▓ **View - Report Manager**

▓ Click the **Add** button.

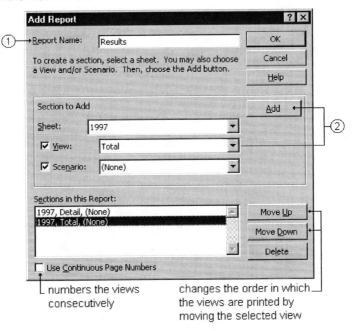

─ numbers the views   changes the order in which ─
consecutively   the views are printed by
                      moving the selected view

① Give the report a name.

② Select each view to be included in the report, then click **Add**.

C-Managing reports

▓ **View - Report Manager**

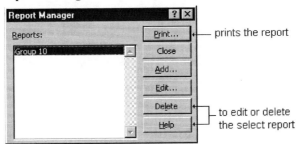

— prints the report

└ to edit or delete
  the select report

7.1 Creating a chart

A-Creating a chart on a sheet

▦ Insert
Chart

▦ Select the chart type and then the sub-type and click the **Next** button.

▦ If all the data that you need for the chart is contained in consecutive cells, select the range in the worksheet then specify whether the series are in **Rows** or **Columns**.

▦ Next open the **Series** page:

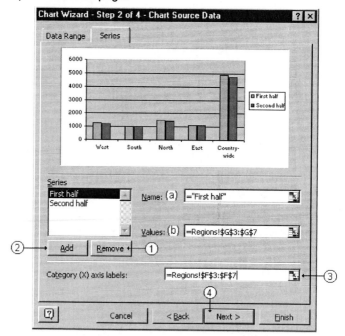

① Delete any series you wish to remove from the chart

② To add a series, click the button, give its name (a), then give the references of the cells containing the values for the series (b).

③ Specify the range of cells which contains the text for the **Category (X)** **labels** or type the text.

④ Go on to the next step.

▦ Give the various titles used in the chart then click **Next>**.

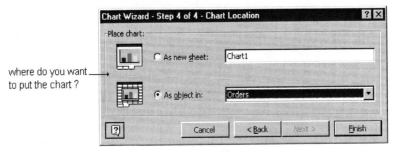

where do you want
to put the chart ?

Click **Finish**.

⇨ *In you chose to insert the chart into a worksheet, it appears in the workspace. Square black handles show that it is selected. This type of chart is known as an **embedded chart**.*

⇨ *To activate an embedded chart click it once: this selects the whole object. To deactivate it, click a cell in the sheet, outside the chart.*

B-Different items in a chart

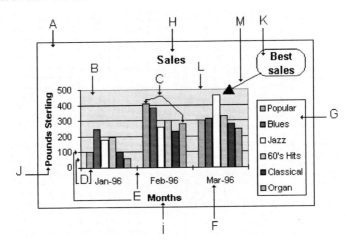

	item	to select
A	Chart area	click in the chart but not in any item
B	Plot area	click in the plot area but not in any item
C	Point	click the series then click the point.
	Series	click one of the data markers in the series
D	Value Axis Category axis	click one of the tick mark labels
E	Tick marks	no selection
F	Tick mark labels	
G	Legend	
H	Chart title	
I	Axis title	
J	Axis title	click the item
K	Text boxes	
L	Gridlines	click one of the lines
M	Arrow	click the item

⇨ *The name of the selected chart item is displayed on the formula bar and in the first list box on the Chart bar.*

C-Setting up the chart for printing

▓ **File - Page Setup**

▓ As well as modifying the usual options, you can adjust the **Printed Chart Size** under the **Chart** tab.

7.2 Chart options

A-Changing the chart type

▓ Chart - Chart type

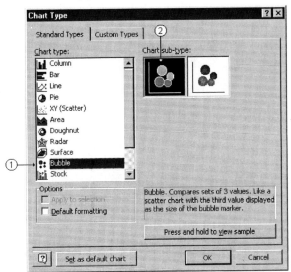

① Choose the chart type.

② Double-click the sub-type you prefer.

⇨ *You can use the* 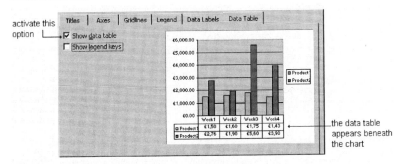 *button on the Chart toolbar to change the chart type but not to choose from the various sub-types.*

B-Displaying the data table

Next to the chart, you can display the table of data on which it is based:

▓ Chart - Chart options
  Data table tab

Microsoft Excel 97

C-Managing pie charts

Rotating a pie chart

▒ Select the series.

▒ **Format**
   Selected data series
   Options tab

⌨ Ctrl 1

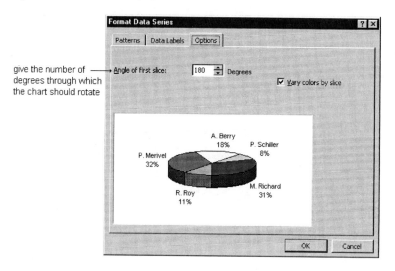

give the number of
degrees through which ───→
the chart should rotate

Exploding a slice

▒ Select the slice you want to explode and drag it away from the rest.

D-Inserting gridlines in a chart

▒ **Chart - Chart options**
   Gridlines tab

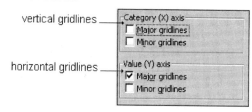

vertical gridlines ──── →

horizontal gridlines ──── →

E-Changing the scale of the chart

▒ Select the value axis.

▒ **Format**
   Selected Axis
   Scale tab

⌨ Ctrl 1

Set the scale options:

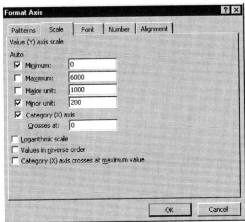

F-Modifying the display of tick mark labels

Select the axis on which the tick mark labels need formatting.

Format
Selected Axis

`Ctrl`1

for formatting the text in the labels ⌐ for orienting the text in the labels

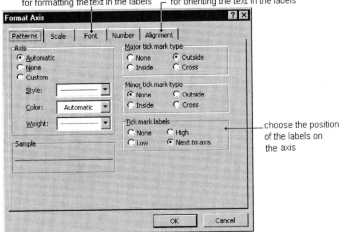

choose the position
of the labels on
the axis

⇨ *With the* ▨ *and* ▨ *buttons on the Chart toolbar you can also change
the orientation of the text in the labels.*

G-Modifying the content of the category labels

Chart - Source data

Change the contents of the **Category (X) labels** box.

Click **OK**.

H-Managing tick marks on the axes

Select the axis concerned.

Format   **1**
Selected Axis
Patterns tab

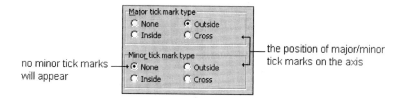

no minor tick marks will appear

the position of major/minor tick marks on the axis

I- Making bars overlap

Select one of the series in the chart.

Format   Ctrl **1**
Selected data series
Options tab

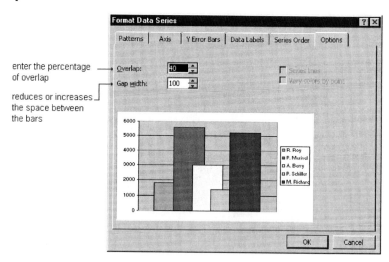

enter the percentage of overlap

reduces or increases the space between the bars

J- Linking points in a line chart

Format   Ctrl **1**
Selected data series
Options tab

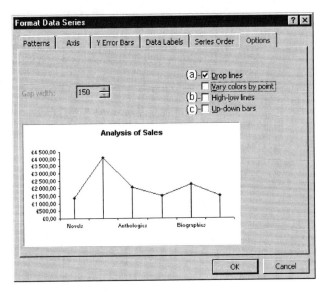

■ Choose between :

(a)   to link points to the category axis.

(b)   to link point to point.

(c)   to use bars to link the points.

K-Adjusting the display of data in 3D charts

■ Chart - 3-D View

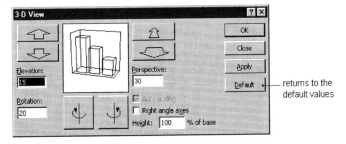

returns to the
default values

7.3 Options for chart items

A-Formatting characters in a chart item

■ Select the characters to be formatted and use the buttons on the Formatting toolbar or click the 🖼 button to define the new format.

The format of numerical values in the chart is defined in the same way.

B-Adding a border/colour/shading to a chart item

Double-click the item concerned.

If necessary, activate the **Patterns** tab.

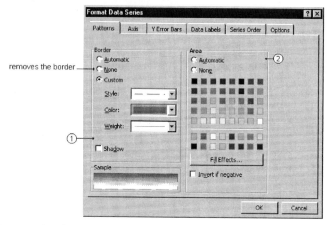

① Choose a border.

② Choose a background colour.

To apply a pattern or a texture to the item, click the **Fill Effects** button.

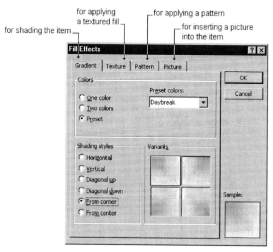

C-Managing chart items

To move or resize an item, select it and drag one of the selection handles to change its dimensions, or one of the borders to move it.

To delete an item, select it and press ⌐Del⌐.

D-Adding text to a chart

A title

▓ **Chart - Chart options**
  Titles tab

give the titles ——→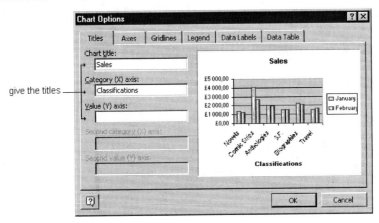

A text linked to a point in a series

▓ Select the point or series concerned.

▓ **Format**
  Selected data or
  Selected data series

  Ctrl 1

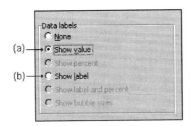

(a) ——→

(b) ——→

▓ Choose (a) or (b) then click **OK**.

▓ If necessary, type in the text you want to appear.

Unattached text (text box)

▓ Make sure that you have not selected any text items.

▓ Type the text required and press Enter .

⇨ *The drawing object created is named Text Box.*

⇨ *To edit the text, select the object (if it is a title or data label), click in the text, modify it and press* Esc .

⇨ *To create a second (third...) line of text, press* Ctrl Enter .

E-Inserting a text from a sheet into a chart

▓ Make sure that you have not selected any item in the chart containing text.

▓ Type =.

▓ Select the cell(s) containing the text to be inserted and enter.

▓ Drag the text box to where you want it.

⇨ *Each time the contents of the cells from the worksheet change, this text will be updated.*

F-Managing legends

▓ To display or hide a legend, click the  button on the **Chart** toolbar.

▓ To determine the legend's position, double-click the legend then activate the **Placement** tab:

```
┌─Type──────────────
│  ○ Bottom
│  ○ Corner
│  ○ Top
│  ⦿ Right
│  ○ Left
```

▓ 7.4 Drawing objects

A-Drawing an object

▓ Display the **Drawing** toolbar (▦).

▓ Click the button corresponding to the shape you want to draw (appendix B includes a description of the Drawing toolbar) or click the **AutoShapes** button then choose one of the shapes proposed.

▓ Drag to draw the object. Hold down the 〔Alt〕 key as you drag to align the shape with the cell gridlines.

⇨ *Hold the* 〔⇧ Shift〕 *key down to draw a perfect circle, square or arc, and for a perfectly straight horizontal, vertical or diagonal line.*

B-Creating a text box

A text box is a drawing object intended to contain text.

27		
28	ANALYSIS	Although they are not among the
29		most expansive items, Classical
30		music cassettes produced the best
31		sales results (V.A.T. included)
32		overall.
33		
34		Note that, in spite of their low price,
35		Soul music cassettes also
36		achieved a very good sales total.
37		
38		

▓ Click 🔲 then drag to draw a text box.

▓ Enter all the text, using ⌨Enter to start new paragraphs.

▓ Press the ⌨Esc key when you have finished.

⇨ *You can go on to format the characters you have entered.*

C-Inserting a ClipArt object

▓ **Insert - Picture - Clip Art**

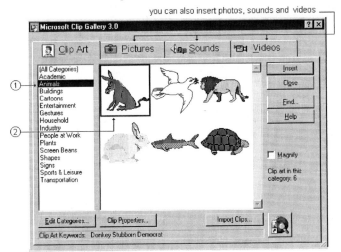

you can also insert photos, sounds and videos

① Select the category to which the object belongs.

② Double-click the object.

*The object is inserted into the worksheet. If it is a drawing object, you can edit it using the tools of the **Picture** bar.*

⇨ The 🔳 button on the **Picture** bar can be used to import the picture contained in a WMF or JPEG... file.

D-Inserting a WordArt object

The WordArt application applies special effects to a text:

Click the ![] button on the **Drawing** toolbar.

Select an effect then click **OK**.

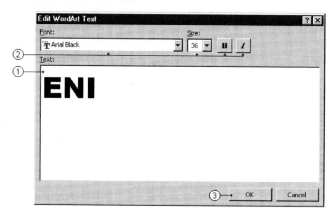

① Type in the text

② Format the text, if appropriate.

③ Create the object.

⇨ *When the text object is selected, you can edit it using the tools from the* **WordArt** *bar.*

E-Managing drawing objects

Click ![].

To select several objects at once, click the first object to select it and hold down the [⇧ Shift] key as you click each of the other objects you want to select.

To delete an object, select it and press [Del].

To resize an object, drag one of the handles which surround it when it is selected.

To move an object, point its border and drag it.

To group a collection of selected objects, click the **Draw** button on the **Drawing** toolbar, then click **Group**. To ungroup objects, use **Draw - Ungroup**.

▓ To change the order of overlapping objects, select the object that you want to bring forward or send further back. Click the **Draw** button then point the **Order** option.

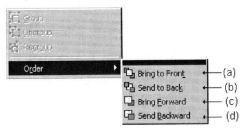

Choose:

(a)   to bring the object to the front.

(b)   to send the object to the back.

(c)   to bring it one place forward.

(d)   to send it one place back.

▓ To align objects with one another, select the objects concerned, click the **Draw** button then choose one of the first six options in the **Align or Distribute** menu.

▓ To rotate objects, select the objects concerned, click the **Draw** button and choose one of the options in the **Rotate or Flip** menu.

F-Changing an object's appearance

A 2D object

▓ Select the object and use the buttons on the **Drawing** toolbar:

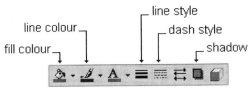

⇨ *The* ▨ *button is used to add arrowheads to line objects.*

A 3D object

▓ Select the object, then click the ▨ button to choose a pre-set 3D style. If none of these styles suit you, click the **3D Settings** button to create a specific 3D effect:

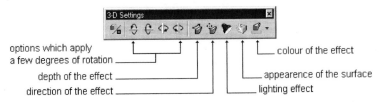

7.5 Series and points

A-Adding/removing a data series

▨ To add a series to an embedded chart, select the data and drag them onto the chart. If the chart is on a chart sheet, copy the data using the clipboard.

▨ To delete a chart, use **Chart - Source Data - Series** tab, select the series and click the **Remove** button.

B-Changing the position of a series

▨ Select one of the series in the chart.

▨ **Format**   **1**
Selected data series
Series Order tab

① Click the series you wish to move.
② Move it in the appropriate direction.

C-Cancelling links between the chart and the worksheet

▨ For each data series :
  » select the series,
  » select all the text in the formula bar,
  » press F9 , and enter.

8.1 Database elements

A- Database vocabulary

▦ Each separate column of data is called a **field**.

fields

Team	Salesmen	Region	Dates	Sales
Lloyd	10	Centre	01/10/92	£100 833.00
Carter	10	West	01/10/92	£104 167.00
Dickson	11	North	01/10/92	£152 500.00
Allsopp	7	South	01/10/92	£83 333.00
Harvey	9	Est	01/10/92	£93 750.00
Lloyd	10	West	01/17/92	£10 400.00
Lloyd	10	Centre	01/17/92	£80 837.00
Carter	10	West	01/17/92	£93 764.00
Allsopp	7	Centre	01/17/92	£20 000.00
Allsopp	7	South	01/17/92	£83 337.00
Harvey	9	Est	01/17/92	£46 875.00
Dickson	11	North	01/17/92	£122 500.00
Dickson	11	North	01/24/92	£100 000.00
Dickson	11	Est	01/24/92	£46 875.00
Lloyd	10	Est	01/24/92	£46 875.00

records

⇨ *When you create a database, you can control the type of data authorised for each field by setting validation rules.*

B-Defining authorised data

▦ Select the cell(s) concerned.
▦ **Data - Validation**
   Settings tab

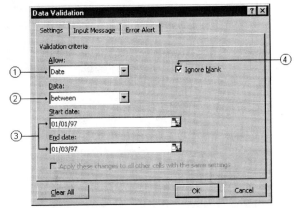

① Choose the type of data you wish to authorise for the cells.
② Select an operator of comparison.

③ Give values for comparison.

④ Deactivate this option to display a message when the cell is left blank.

▨ Click the **Error Alert** tab to set the following options:

Style The warning symbol which will appear in the dialog box containing the error message.

Title The title of the dialog box.

Error Message The text of the message.

▨ Click **OK**.

⇨ *Data entered before the criteria were set are not tested (Excel can, however, trace unauthorised data and circle the cells which contain it in red: to exploit this option, click the ▦ button on the Auditing toolbar).*

⇨ *The options on the Input Message page of the Data Validation dialog box, make it possible to display a message in a ScreenTip when the mouse pointer is on the cell.*

C-Using the data form

Going into the data form

▨ Click a cell in a table designed as a data base.

▨ **Data - Form**

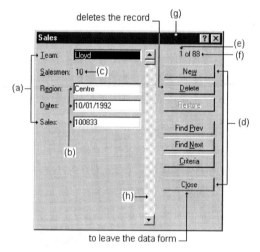

(a) Field names

(b) Edit boxes for entering field contents

(c) Data form fields containing computed fields

(d) Command buttons

(e) (f) The number of the current record and the total number of records

(g) Title bar

(h)   Vertical scroll bar

D-Managing records

- To add a record, click the **New** button; fill in the new record pressing 〔⇄〕 or 〔⇧ Shift〕〔⇄〕 to move from box to box.
- Press 〔Enter〕 to confirm the data you have typed.
- To move from record to record, use the scroll bar, or the arrow keys:

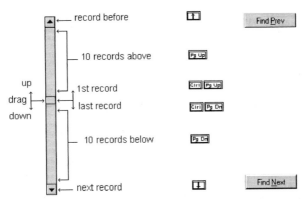

- To edit a record, access it, make the necessary changes then press 〔Enter〕 (the **Restore** button retrieves the former values).

⇨ *The last form displayed is always a new form ready to be filled in.*

Going to a particular record

- Display either the first or last record.
- Click the **Criteria** button.
- Enter the search criteria in the same way as you would fill in a record but without pressing 〔Enter〕.

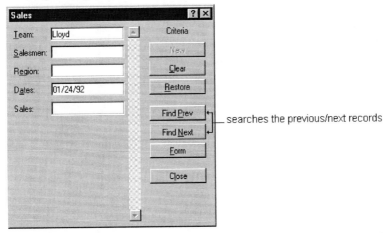

searches the previous/next records

E-Sorting records

■ Data - Sort

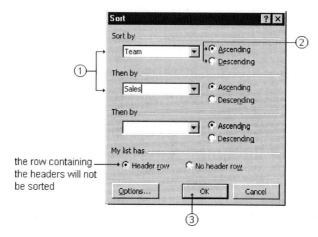

① Choose the fields by which you want to sort (data is sorted by the second field when the values in the first field are identical).

② For each field, give the sort order.

③ Sort the data.

8.2 Filters

A-Creating and using a simple filter

Using a filter, you can select records corresponding to a particular criterion.

■ Data - Filter - AutoFilter

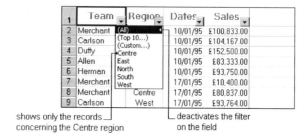

shows only the records ‒ deactivates the filter
concerning the Centre region on the field

Each field becomes a drop-down list which opens when you click the down arrow.

To filter by one of the values listed, open the list associated with the field concerned and click the value.

Filtering the highest and lowest values

Open the field concerned and click (**Top 10...**).

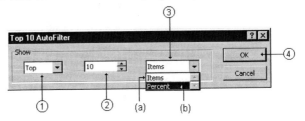

① Indicate whether you want top values or bottom values.

② Specify how many of the top/bottom values you wish to see.

③ Choose:

(a) to filter all the records corresponding to the criteria (top or bottom)

(b) to filter a number of rows corresponding to a percentage of the total number of values in the list

④ Apply the filter.

Filtering by several criteria

Click **Custom** in the list for the field concerned.

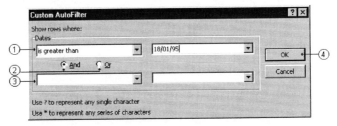

① Give the operator and the value which make up the first filter criterion.

② Choose **And** if both criteria must be satisfied together.
Choose **Or** if either one or the other must be satisfied.

③ Enter the second condition.

④ Apply the filter.

⇨ *To combine criteria relating to several fields and connected with the "and" operator, enter the conditions in each field concerned.*

⇨ *To display all the records again, use the command **Data - Filter - Show All**.*

B-Filtering by complex criteria

Creating a criteria range

In a space on the worksheet type a first row made up of the names of the fields to be used in the filter criteria and in the rows below, type the criteria:

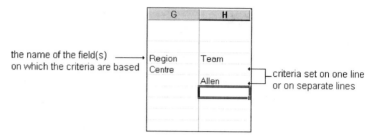

The criteria must be set out as follows:

combination	method
OR	the criteria are entered in several rows
AND	the criteria are entered in several columns
AND and OR	the criteria are entered in several rows and several columns

The examples below will help :

Requirements	Criteria ranges	
Records concerning Central, Western and Southern regions : Central region OR Western region OR Southern region	**Region**	
	Centre	
	West	
	South	
Central Region records made by Lloyd : Central Region AND Lloyd's team	**Region**	**Team**
	Centre	Lloyd
Central Region records made by Lloyd or Allen or Carter: Central Region AND (Lloyd's team OR Allen's team OR Carter's team)	**Region**	**Team**
	Centre	Lloyd
	Centre	Allen
	Centre	Carter

⇨ *To extract MARTIN but not MARTINEZ, MARTINELLI..., enter the criteria ="=MARTIN".*

Using a criteria range to filter records

▦ Click inside the database and run the command:
Data - Filter - Advanced Filter

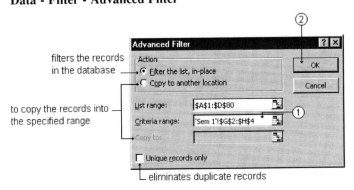

filters the records
in the database

to copy the records into
the specified range

eliminates duplicate records

① Click here then select the criteria range on the worksheet.

② Apply the filter.

⇨ *To copy the records which meet the filter criteria, the first row of the destination range (whose location is given in the **Copy to** box) must contain the names of the fields to filter.*

C-Calculating statistics from the records

▦ Create the appropriate criteria range then use the following functions:

Function	Effect
=DCOUNT(database,field,criteria)	counts the cells
=DSUM(database,field,criteria)	totals the values of the field
=DAVERAGE(database,field,criteria)	calculates the average for the field
=DMAX(database,field,criteria)	extracts the maximal value in the field
=DMIN(database,field,criteria)	extracts the minimal value in the field

database	the reference of the cells containing the list of records (including column headings).
field	the column heading.
criteria	either the word **criteria** if you have created a complex filter or the references of the cells containing the criteria range.

8.3 Pivot tables

A-Making a Pivot table

A pivot table allows you to synthesise and analyse data from a list or an existing table :

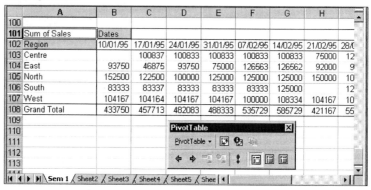

	A	B	C	D	E	F	G	H	
100									
101	Sum of Sales	Dates							
102	Region	10/01/95	17/01/95	24/01/95	31/01/95	07/02/95	14/02/95	21/02/95	28/0
103	Centre		100837	100833	100833	100833	100833	75000	12
104	East	93750	46875	93750	75000	126563	126562	92000	9
105	North	152500	122500	100000	125000	125000	125000	150000	10
106	South	83333	83337	83333	83333	83333	125000		12
107	West	104167	104164	104167	104167	100000	108334	104167	10
108	Grand Total	433750	457713	482083	488333	535729	585729	421167	55
109									
110									
111									
112									
113									

This table calculates total sales by region and by date.

Data
PivotTable Report

Indicate the source of the data for the pivot table then click **Next>**.

Select the cells containing the data used to fill in the table then click **Next>**.

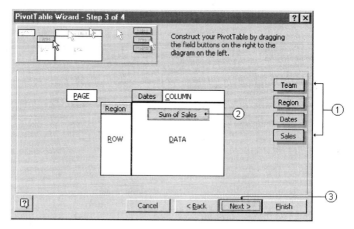

Construct your PivotTable by dragging the field buttons on the right to the diagram on the left.

① Drag the field buttons from the list into the appropriate areas (**PAGE, ROW, COLUMN, DATA**).

② Double-click the appropriate button to customise the characteristics of the field.

③ Move on to the next stage.

Indicate whether the pivot table should be created on a new sheet or in an existing sheet then click **Finish**.

⇨ *To modify a pivot table, click inside the table and go through the procedure that you used to create it.*

⇨ *To update the data in the pivot table, click the* ▨ *button on the* **Pivot Table** *toolbar.*

B-Grouping rows or columns in the table

▨ Click the name of the field by which you intend to group the data.

▨ Click the ▨ button to define how the data is grouped.

⇨ *To ungroup the data click the field name then click* ▨.

DATABASE

9.1 Macros

A-Creating a macro

If necessary, open the workbook concerned by the macro.

Tools - Macros - Record New Macro.

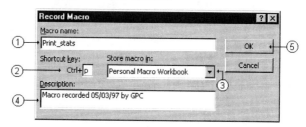

① Give the macro a name.

② If you wish, specify a shortcut key which will run the macro.

③ Indicate where the macro is to be stored: if you want the macro to be permanently accessible, choose **Personal macro Workbook**.

④ Make any necessary changes to the description of the macro.

⑤ Start to record the macro.

Go through all the actions to be automated in the macro.

When all the actions have been recorded, click the [■] button on the Stop Rec. bar.

⇨ *Macros recorded in this way are created in a file called PERSONAL.XLS, where all personal macros are stored. This type of macro is always accessible as the Personal file is automatically opened when Excel is started.*

B-Running a macro

If a macro has been created in a workbook other than PERSONAL.XLS, open it.

Tools - Macro - Macros (or [Alt][F8])

Double-click the macro you want to run.

⇨ *You could also press the shortcut key defined when the macro was created.*

C-Opening an Add-In

These macros are provided with Excel but are not automatically loaded.

Tools - Add-Ins

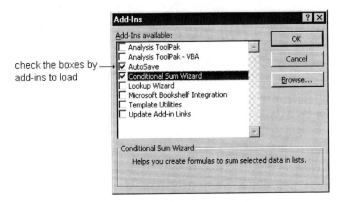

check the boxes by add-ins to load

⇨ *Add-ins appear as options in different Excel menus.*

D-Viewing the contents of a macro

▓ If the macro is stored in PERSONAL.XLS, use the command **Window - Unhide** to display it, as you would for any other hidden workbook.

▓ **Tools - Macro - Macros** (or [Alt][F8])

▓ Select the macro, then click **Edit**.

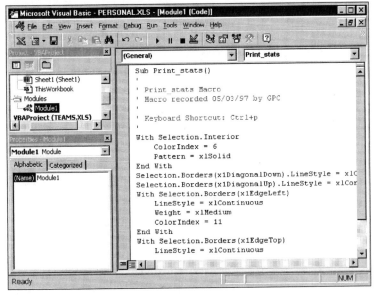

The contents of the macro, written in Visual Basic appear.

WORKING WITH MENUS

Display shortcut menu ⇧ Shift F10

Document window Control menu

Restore window size Ctrl F5
Carry out move command Ctrl F7
Carry out size command Ctrl F8
Minimize window Ctrl F9

Maximize window Ctrl F10
Close window Ctrl F4 or Ctrl W
Switch to next
window Ctrl ⇄

Application window Control menu

Close Window Alt F4
Start menu Ctrl Esc

File

New Ctrl N
Open Ctrl O
Save Ctrl S

Save As F12
Print Ctrl P
Exit Alt F4

Edit

Undo Ctrl Z
Repeat Ctrl Y
Cut Ctrl X
Copy Ctrl C
Paste Ctrl V
   Fill down Ctrl D
   Fill right Ctrl R

Clear contents Del
Delete Ctrl -
Find Ctrl F
   Next ⇧ Shift F4
   Previous Ctrl ⇧ Shift F4
Replace Ctrl H
Go To F5 or Ctrl G

Insert

Cells, Rows, Columns Ctrl +
Worksheet ⇧ Shift F11
Chart
   As New Sheet F11

Names
   Define Ctrl F3
   Paste F3
   Create Ctrl ⇧ Shift F3
Cell comment ⇧ Shift F2

Format

Cells, Object Ctrl 1
Row
   Hide Ctrl 9
   Unhide Ctrl ⇧ Shift (

Columns
   Hide Ctrl 0
   Unhide Ctrl ⇧ Shift)
Style Alt '

Tools

Spelling F7
Macro
   Macros Alt F8
   Visual Basic Editor Alt F11

Calculation
   Calc. Now F9
   Calc. Sheet ⇧ Shift F9

Data

Group and Outline
Group   `Alt` `⇧ Shift` `→`
Ungroup   `Alt` `⇧ Shift` `←`

Help

Microsoft Excel Help   `F1`
What is it?   `⇧ Shift` `F1`

OTHER KEY COMBINATIONS

Individual data

Enter the date	`Ctrl` ;	Insert Autosum formula	`Alt` =
Enter the time	`Ctrl` `⇧ Shift` :	Insert matrix formula	`Ctrl` `⇧ Shift` `Enter`
Insert formula in cell above	`Ctrl` '	Clear the selection of	
Insert value of cell above	`Ctrl` `⇧ Shift` "	formulas and data	`Del`
Insert a line break	`Alt` `Enter`	Insert a hyperlink	`Ctrl` K
		Display list of AutoComplete entries	`Alt` `↓`

Working in the Formula Bar

Activate a cell and the formula bar	`F 2`	Delete from insertion point to the end of line	`Ctrl` `Del`
Start a formula	=	Cancel a cell entry	`Esc`
		Validate a cell entry	`Enter`
Enter in selected cells			`Ctrl` `Enter`
Relative and absolute references			`F 4`
After a function, displays formula palette			`Ctrl` A
After a function, displays arguments			`Ctrl` `⇧ Shift` A

Formatting cells

Apply outline	`Ctrl` `⇧ Shift` &	Italics	`Ctrl` I
Remove all borders	`Ctrl` `⇧ Shift` -	Underline	`Ctrl` U
Bold format	`Ctrl` B	Display font list	`Ctrl` `⇧ Shift` P

Formatting numbers and dates

Normal number format	`Ctrl` `⇧ Shift` ~
Two decimal places (0.00)	`Ctrl` `⇧ Shift` !
Currency format with two decimal places (# ##£0.00)	`Ctrl` `⇧ Shift` $
Exponential number format with two decimal places (0.00E + 00)	`Ctrl` `⇧ Shift` ^
Date format (dd/mm/yy)	`Ctrl` `⇧ Shift` #
Time format (h:mm AM/PM)	`Ctrl` `⇧ Shift` @

SHORTCUT KEYS

In Outline mode

Ungroup a row or column   `Alt` `⇧ Shift` `←`
Group a row or column   `Alt` `⇧ Shift` `→`
Unhide/hide the outline symbols   `Ctrl` 8

Display

Unhide/hide the standard toolbar   `Ctrl` 7

Selections

Select the entire worksheet   `Ctrl` A   Extend the selection   `F8`
Select the entire column   `Ctrl` `space`   Add to the selection   `⇧ Shift` `F8`
Select the entire row   `⇧ Shift` `space`

Selection of individual cells

Select cells containing comments   `Control` `⇧ Shift` O
Select rectangular array of cells surrounding the active cell   `Ctrl` `⇧ Shift` *
Select the entire array to which the cell belongs   `Ctrl` /
Select only cells to which the formulas in the selection
make direct reference   `Ctrl` [
Select all cells to which formulas in the selection
make direct or indirect reference   `Ctrl` `⇧ Shift` {
Select only cells with formulas that refer directly or to the active cell   `Ctrl`]
Select all cells with formulas that refer directly or indirectly
to the active cell   `Ctrl` `⇧ Shift` }
Select only visible cells in the current selection   `Alt` ;
Select cells whose contents are different from the comparison cell
in each row. For each row the comparison cell is in the same column
as the active cell   `Ctrl` \
Select cells whose contents are different from the comparison cell
in each column. For each column the comparison cell is in the same
row as the active cell   `Ctrl` `⇧ Shift` |

Moving from one window to another

Display the next window   `Ctrl` `F6` or `Ctrl` `⇄`
Display the previous window   `Ctrl` `⇧ Shift` `F6` or `Ctrl` `⇧ Shift` `⇄`

Moving around a workbook

Move to the next sheet in the workbook   `Ctrl` `Pg Dn`
Move to the previous sheet in the workbook   `Ctrl` `Pg Up`
Go to the next pane   `F6`
Go to the previous pane   `⇧ Shift` `F6`

Standard Toolbar

1	New workbook	12	Redo
2	Open	13	Insert hyperlink
3	Save	14	Web toolbar
4	Print	15	AutoSum
5	Print preview	16	Paste function
6	Spelling	17	Sort ascending
7	Cut	18	Sort descending
8	Copy	19	Chart Wizard
9	Paste	20	Map
10	Format painter	21	Drawing
11	Undo	22	Zoom
		23	Office Assistant

Formatting Toolbar

1	Font	10	Currency style
2	Font size	11	Percentage
3	Bold	12	Comma style
4	Italic	13	Increase decimal
5	Underline	14	Decrease decimal
6	Align left	15	Increase indent
7	Center	16	Decrease indent
8	Align right	17	Borders
9	Merge and centre	18	Fill colour
		19	Font colour

Chart Toolbar

1	Chart objects list	6	By row
2	Format selected object	7	By column
3	Chart type	8	Angle text downward
4	Legend	9	Angle text upward
5	Data table		

TOOLBARS

Drawing Toolbar

1	Draw menu	10	Insert WordArt
2	Select objects	11	Fill colour
3	Free rotate	12	Line colour
4	Autoshapes menu	13	Font colour
5	Line	14	Line style
6	Arrow	15	Dash style
7	Rectangle	16	Arrow style
8	Oval	17	Shadow
9	Text Box	18	3D

Reviewing Toolbar

1	New comment	6	Delete comments
2	Previous comment	7	Create Microsoft Outlook task
3	Next comment	8	Update file
4	Show comment	9	Send to mail recipient
5	Show all comments		

Audit Toolbar

1	Trace precedents	5	Remove all arrows
2	Remove precedent arrows	6	Trace error
3	Trace dependents	7	Attach notes
4	Remove dependent arrows	8	Show info window
		9	Clear validation circles

Picture Toolbar

1	Insert picture from file	7	Crop
2	Image control	8	Line style
3	More contrast	9	Format object
4	Less contrast	10	Set transparent colour
5	More brightness	11	Reset picture
6	Less brightness		

WordArt Toolbar

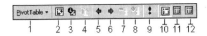

1	Insert WordArt	6	Free rotate
2	Edit text	7	WordArt same letter heights
3	WordArt gallery	8	WordArt vertical text
4	Format object	9	WordArt alignment
5	WordArt shape	10	WordArt character spacing

PivotTable Toolbar

1	PivotTable menu	7	Hide detail
2	PivotTable Wizard	8	Show detail
3	PivotTable field	9	Refresh data
4	Show pages	10	Select label
5	Ungroup	11	Select data
6	Group	12	Select label and data

TOOLBARS

FINANCIAL FUNCTIONS

cost	*the initial cost of the asset*
salvage	*the value at the end of the depreciation*
life	*the number of periods over which the asset is being depreciated*
pv	*present value that a series of future payments is worth right now*
fv	*the future value, or the cash balance obtained after the last payment; if it is omitted, it is assumed to be 0*
Type	*indicates when payments are due. If it is 0 (or omitted), the payments are due at the end of the period. If 1, they are due at the beginning*
rate	*the interest rate per period*
nper	*the number of periods for an investissment based on periodic, constant payments and a constant interest rate*
pmt	*the payment made each period*
period	*the period for which you want to calculate the depreciation. This argument must use the same unit as life*
DB	*(cost,salvage,life,period)* Returns the depreciation of an asset for a specified period using the fixed-declining balance method.
DDB	*(cost,salvage,life,period)* Returns the depreciation of an asset for a specified period using the double-declining balance method or some other method you specify.
FV	*(rate,nper,pmt)* Returns the future value of an investment.
IPMT	*(rate,per,nper,pv)* Returns the interest payment for an investment for a given period.
IRR	*(values)* Returns the internal rate of return for a series of cash flows.
MIRR	*(finance_rate,reinvest_rate)* Returns the internal rate of return where positive and negative cash flows are financed at different rates.
NPER	*(rate,pmt,pv)* Returns the number of periods for an investment.
NPV	*(rate,value1,value2...)* Returns the net present value of an investment based on a series of periodic cash flows and a discount rate.
PMT	*(rate,nper)* Returns the periodic payment for an annuity.
PPMT	*(rate,nper)* Returns the payment on the principal for an investment for a given period.
PV	*(rate,nper,pmt)* Returns the present value of an investment.
RATE	*(nper,pmt,pv)* Returns the interest rate per period of an annuity.
SLN	*(cost,salvage,life)* Returns the straight-line depreciatioin of an asset for one period.
SYD	*(cost,salvage,life,period)* Returns the sum-of-years' digits depreciation of an asset for a specified period. Returns the yield for a Treasury bill.
VDB	*(cost,salvage,life,start_period,end_period)* Returns the depreciation of an asset for a specified or partial period using a declining balance method.

DATE AND TIME FUNCTIONS

The digits to the left of a serial_number represent dates, those on the right represent the time. Date serial numbers are between 1 and 65380 : the 1st of January 1900 and the 31th of December 2078.

DATE	*(year,month,day)*	Returns the serial number of a particular date.
DATEVALUE	*(date_text)*	Converts a date in the form of text to a serial number.
DAY	*(serial_n°)*	Converts a serial number to a day of the month.
DAY360	*(start_date,end_date,method)*	Calculates the number of days between two dates based on a 360-day year.
HOUR	*(serial_n°)*	Converts a serial number to an hour.
MINUTE	*(serial_n°)*	Converts a serial number to a minute.
MONTH	*(serial_n°)*	Converts a serial number to a month.
NOW	*()*	Returns the serial number of the current date and time.
SECOND	*(serial_n°)*	Converts a serial number to a second.
TIME	*(hour,min,sec)*	Returns the serial number of a particular time.
TIMEVALUE	*(time_text)*	Converts a time in the form of text to a serial number.
TODAY	*()*	Returns the serial number of today's date.
WEEKDAY	*(serial_n°,return_type)*	Converts a serial number to a day of the week.
YEAR	*(serial_n°)*	Converts a serial number to a year.

MATH AND TRIGONOMETRY FUNCTIONS

ABS	*(number)*	Returns the absolute value of a number.
ACOS	*(number)*	Returns the arccosine of a number.
ACOSH	*(number)*	Returns the inverse hyperbolic cosine of a number.
ASIN	*(number)*	Returns the arcsine of a number.
ASINH	*(number)*	Returns the inverse hyperbolic sine of a number.
ATAN	*(number)*	Returns the arctangent of a number.
ATAN2	*(x_num,y_num)*	Returns the arctangent of x- and y- coordinates.
ATANH	*(number)*	Returns the inverse hyperbolic tangent of a number.

CEILING	*(number,signifiance)*
	Rounds a number to the nearest integer or to the nearest multiple of significance.
COMBIN	*(number,number_chosen)*
	Returns the number of combinations for a given number of objects.
COS	*(number)*
	Returns the cosine of a number.
COSH	*(number)*
	Returns the hyperbolic cosine of a number.
COUNTBLANK	*(range)*
	Counts the number of blank cells within a range.
COUNTIF	*(range,criteria)*
	Counts the number of non-blank cells within a range which meet the given criteria.
DEGREES	*(angle)*
	Converts radians to degrees.
EVEN	*(number)*
	Rounds a number up to the nearest even integer.
EXP	*(number)*
	Returns e raised to the power of a given number.
FACT	*(number)*
	Returns the factorial of a number.
FLOOR	*(number,signifiance)*
	Rounds a number down, toward zero.
INT	*(number)*
	Rounds a number down to the nearest integer.
LCM	*(number1,number2...)*
	Returns the least common multiple.
LN	*(number)*
	Returns the natural logarithm of a number.
LOG	*(number,base)*
	Returns the logarithm of a number to a specified base.
LOG10	*(number)*
	Returns the base -10 logarithm of a number.
MDETERM	*(array)*
	Returns the matrix determinant of an array.
MINVERSE	*(array)*₌
	Returns the matrix inverse of an array.
MMULT	*(array1,array2)*
	Returns the matrix product of two arrays.
MOD	*(number,divisor)*
	Returns the remainder from division.
ODD	*(number)*
	Rounds a number up to the nearest odd integer.
PI	*()*
	Returns the value of Pi.
POWER	*(number,power)*
	Returns the result of a number raised to a power.
PRODUCT	*(number1,number2,...)*
	Multiplies its arguments.
RADIANS	*(angle)*
	Converts degrees to radians.

RAND	*()* Returns a random number between 0 and 1.
ROMAN	*(number,form)* Converts an Arabic numeral to Roman, as text.
ROUND	*(number,number_digits)* Rounds a number to a specified number of digits.
ROUNDDOWN	*(number,num_digits)* Rounds a number down, toward zero.
ROUNDUP	*(number,num_digits)* Rounds a number up, away from zero.
SIGN	*(number)* Returns the sign of a number.
SIN	*(number)* Returns the sine of the given angle.
SINH	*(number)* Returns the hyperbolic siine of a number.
SQRT	*(number)* Returns a positive square root.
SUM	*(number1,number2,...)* Adds its arguments.
SUMIF	*(range,criteria,sum_range)* Adds the cells specified by a given criteria.
SUMPRODUCT	*(array1,array2)* Returns the sum of the products of corresponding array components.
SUMSQ	*(number1,number2,....)* Returns the sum of the squares of the arguments.
SUMX2MY2	*(array_x,array_y)* Returns the sum of the difference of squares of corresponding values in two arrays.
SUMX2PY2	*(array_x,array_y)* Returns the sum of the sum of squares of corresponding values in two arrays.
SUMXMY2	*(array_x,array_y)* Returns the sum of squares of differences of corresponding values in two arrays.
TAN	*(number)* Returns the tangent of a number.
TANH	*(number)* Returns the hyperbolic tangent of a number.
TRUNC	*(number,num_digits)* Truncates a number to an integer.

STATISTICAL FUNCTIONS

AVEDEV	*(number1,number2,...)* Returns the average of the absolute deviations of data points from their mean.
AVERAGE	*(number1,number2,...)* Returns the average of its arguments.
AVERAGEA	*(number1,number2...)* Returns the average value of a range of cells, including in the calculation cells which contain text, or the values TRUE or FALSE.
BETADIST	*(x,alpha,beta,A,B)* Returns the cumulative beta probability density function.

BETAINV	*(probability,alpha,beta,A,B)* Returns the inverse of the cumulative beta probability density function.
BINOMDIST	*(number_s,trials,probability_s,cumulative)* Returns the individual term binomial distribution probability.
CHIDIST	*(x,degrees_freedom)* Returns the one-tailed probability of the chi-squared distribution.
CHIINV	*(probability,degrees_freedom)* Returns the inverse of the one-tailed probability of the chi-squared distribution.
CHITEST	*(actual_range,expected_range)* Returns the test for independence.
CONFIDENCE	*(alpha,standard_dev,size)* Returns the confidence interval for a population mean.
CORREL	*(array1,array2)* Returns the correlation coefficient between two data sets.
COUNT	*(value1,value2,...)* Counts how many numbers are in the list of arguments.
COUNTA	*(value1,value2,...)* Counts how many values are in the list of arguments.
COVAR	*(array1,array2)* Returns covariance, the average of the products of paired deviations.
CRITBINOM	*(trials,probability_s,alpha)* Returns the smallest value for which the cumulative binomial distribution is less than or equal to a criterion value.
DEVSQ	*(number1,number2...)* Returns the sum of squares of deviations.
EXPONDIST	*(x,lambda,cumulative)* Returns the exponential distribution.
FDIST	*(x,degrees_freedom1,degrees_freedom2)* Returns the F probability distribution.
FINV	*(probability,degrees_freedom1,degrees_freedom2)* Returns the inverse of the F probability distribution.
FISHER	*(x)* Returns the Fisher transformation.
FISHERINV	*(y)* Returns the inverse of the Fisher transformation.
FORECAST	*(x,known_y's,known_x's)* Returns a value along a linear trend.
FREQUENCY	*(data_array,bins_array)* Returns a frequency distribution as a vertical array.
FTEST	*(array1,array2)* Returns the result of an F-test.
GAMMADIST	*(x,alpha,beta,cumulative)* Returns the gamma distribution.
GAMMAINV	*(probability,alpha,beta)* Returns the inverse of the gamma cumulative distribution.
GAMMALN	*(x)* Returns the natural logarithm of the gamma function, Γ or $\diamond(X)$.
GEOMEAN	*(number1,number2,...)* Returns the geometric mean.
GROWTH	*(known_y's,known_x's,new_x's,const)* Returns values along an exponential trend.

HARMEAN	(number1,number2,...)
	Returns the harmonic mean.
HYPGEOMDIST	(sample_s,number_sample,populatoin_s,number_population)
	Returns the hypergeometric distribution.
INTERCEPT	(known_y's,known_x's)
	Returns the intercept of the linear regression line.
KURT	(number1,number2,...)
	Returns the kurtosis of a data set.
LARGE	(array,k)
	Returns the k-th largest value in a data set.
LINEST	(known_y's,known_x's,const,stats)
	Returns the parameters of a linear trend.
LOGEST	(known_y's,known_x's,const,stats)
	Returns the parameters of an exponential trend.
LOGINV	(probability,mean,standard_dev)
	Returns the inverse of the lognormal distribution.
LOGNORMDIST	(x,mean,standard_dev)
	Returns the cumulative lognormal distribution.
MAX	(number1,number2,...)
	Returns the maximum value in a list of arguments.
MAXA	(number1, number2,...)
	Returns the maximum value in a range of cells, including in the calculation cells which contain text or the values TRUE or FALSE.
MEDIAN	(number1,number2,...)
	Returns the median of the given numbers.
MIN	(number1,number2,...)
	Returns the minimum value in a list of arguments.
MINA	(number1,number2,...)
	Returns the minimum value in a range of cells, including in the calculation cells which contain text or the values TRUE or FALSE.
MODE	(number1,number2,...)
	Returns the most common value in a data set.
NEGBINOMDIST	(number_f,number_s,probability_s)
	Returns the negative binomial distribution.
NORMDIST	(x,mean,standard_dev,cumulative)
	Returns the standard normal cumulative distribution.
NORMINV	(probability,mean,standard_dev)
	Returns the inverse of the normal cumulative distribution.
NORMSDIST	(Z)
	Returns the standard normal cumulative distribution.
NORMSINV	(probability)
	Returns the inverse of the standard normal cumulative distribution.
PEARSON	(array1,array2)
	Returns the Pearson product moment correlation coefficient.
PERCENTILE	(array,k)
	Returns the k-th percentile of values in a range.
PERCENTRANK	(array,k,signifiance)
	Returns the percentage rank of a value in a data set.
PERMUT	(number,number_chosen)
	Returns the number of permutations for a given number of objects.
POISSON	(x,mean,cumulative)
	Returns the Poisson distribution.

INTEGRATED FUNCTIONS

PROB	*(x_range,prob_range,lower_limit,upper_limit)*
	Returns the probability that values in a range are between two limits.
QUARTILE	*(array,quart)*
	Returns the quartile of a data set.
RANK	*(number,ref,order)*
	Returns the rank of a number in a list of numbers.
SKEW	*(number1,number2,...)*
	Returns the skewness of a distribution.
SLOPE	*(known_y's,known_x's)*
	Returns the slope of the liner regression line.
SMALL	*(array,k)*
	Returns the k-th smallest value in a data set.
STANDARDIZE	*(x,mean,standard_dev)*
	Returns a normalized value.
STDEV	*(number1,number2,...)*
	Estimates standard deviation based on a sample.
STDEVA	*(number1,number2...)*
	Estimates standard deviation based on a sample of the population, including in the calculation ...
STDEVP	*(number1,number2,...)*
	Calculates standard deviation based on the entire population.
STDEVPA	*(number1,number2...)*
	Calculates standard deviation based on the entire population, including ...
STEYX	*(known_y's,known_x's)*
	Returns the standard error of the predicted y-value for each x in the regression.
TDIST	*(x,degrees_freedom,tails)*
	Returns the Studen's t-distribution.
TINV	*(probability,degrees_freedom)*
	Returns the inverse of the Student's t-distribution.
TREND	*(known_y's,known_x's,new_x's,const)*
	Returns values along a linear trend.
TRIMMEAN	*(array,percent)*
	Returns the mean of the interior of a data set.
TTEST	*(array1,array2,tails,type)*
	Returns the probability associated with a Student's t-Test.
VAR	*(number1,number2,...)*
	Estimates variance based on a sample.
VARA	*(number1,number2,...)*
	Estimates variance based on a sample, including ...
VARP	*(number1,number2,...)*
	Calculates variance based on the entire population.
VARPA	*(number1,number2,...)*
	Calculates variance based on a sample including ...
WEIBULL	*(x,alpha,beta,cumulative)*
	Returns the Weibull distribution.
ZTEST	*(array,x,sigma)*
	Returns the two-tailed P-value of a z-test.

LOOKUP AND REFERENCE FUNCTIONS

ADDRESS *(row_num,column_num,abs_num,a1,sheet_text)*
Returns a reference as text to a single cell in a worksheet.

AREAS *(reference)*
Returns the number of areas in a reference.

CHOOSE *(index_num,value1,value2)*
Chooses a value from a list of values.

COLUMN *(reference)*
Returns the column number of a reference.

COLUMNS *(array)*
Returns the number of columns in a reference.

HLOOKUP *(lookup_value,table_array,row_index_num,range_lookup)*
Looks in the top row of an array and returns the value of the indicated cell.

INDEX *(...)*
Uses an index to choose a value from a reference or array.

INDIRECT *(ref_text,a1)*
Returns a reference indicated by a text value.

HYPERLINK *(link_location,friendly_name)*
Creates a shortcut that opens a document stored on a network server, an intranet or the Internet.

LOOKUP *(...)*
Looks up values in a vector or array.

MATCH *(lookup_value,lookup_array,match_type)*
Looks up values in a reference or array.

OFFSET *(reference,rows,cols,height,width)*
Returns a reference offset from a given reference.

ROW *(reference)*
Returns the number of a reference.

ROWS *(array)*
Returns the number of rows in a reference.

TRANSPOSE *(array)*
Returns the transpose of an array.

VLOOKUP *(lookup_value,table_array,col_index_num,range_lookup)*
Looks in the first column of an array and moves across the row to return the value of a cell.

DATABASE FUNCTIONS

DAVERAGE *(database,field,criteria)*
Returns the average of selected database entries.

DCOUNT *(database,field,criteria)*
Counts the cells containing numbers from a specified database and criteria.

DCOUNTA *(database,field,criteria)*
Counts nonblank cells from a specified database and criteria.

DGET *(database,field,criteria)*
Extracts from a database a single record that matches the specified criteria.

DMAX *(database,field,criteria)*
Returns the maximum value from selected database entries.

DMIN *(database,field,criteria)*
Returns the minimum value from selected database entries.

DPRODUCT	*(database,field,criteria)* Multiplies the values in a particular field of records that match the criteria in a database.
DSTDEV	*(database,field,criteria)* Estimates the standard deviation based on a sample of selected database entries.
DSTDEVP	*(database,field,criteria)* Calculates the standard deviation based on the entire population of selected database entries.
DSUM	*(database,field,criteria)* Adds the numbers in the field column of records in the database that match the criteria.
DVAR	*(database,field,criteria)* Estimates variance based on a sample from selected database entries.
DVARP	*(database,field,criteria)* Calculates variance based on the entire population of selected database entries.
GETPIVOTDATA	*(pivot_table,name)* Returns data stored in a PivotTable.

TEXT FUNCTIONS

CHAR	*(number)* Returns the character specified by the code number.
CLEAN	*(text)* Removes all nonprintable characters from text.
CODE	*(text)* Returns a numeric code for the first character in a text string.
CONCATENATE	*(text1,text2,...)* Joins several text items into one text item.
DOLLAR	*(number,decimals)* Converts a number to text, using currency format.
EXACT	*(text)* Checks to see if two text values are identical.
FIND	*(find_text,within_text,start_num)* Finds one text value within another (case-sensitive).
FIXED	*(number,decimals,no_commas)* Formats a number as text with a fixed number of decimals.
LEFT	*(text,num_chars)* Returns the leftmost characters from a text value.
LEN	*(text)* Returns the number of characters in a text string.
LOWER	*(text)* Converts text to lowercase.
MID	*(text,start_num,num_chars)* Returns a specific number of characters from a text string starting at the position you specify.
PROPER	*(text)* Capitalizes the first letter in each word of a text value.
REPLACE	*(old_text,start_num,num_chars,new_text)* Replaces characters within text.
REPT	*(text,number_times)* Repeats text a given number of times.

RIGHT	*(text,num_chars)*
	Returns the rightmost characters from a text value.
SEARCH	*(find_text,within_text,start_num)*
	Finds one text value within another (not case-sensitive).
SUBSTITUTE	*(text,old_text,new_text,instance_num)*
	Substitutes new text for old text in a text string.
T	*(value)*
	Converts its arguments to text.
TEXT	*(value,format_text)*
	Formats a number and converts it to text.
TRIM	*(text)*
	Removes spaces from text.
UPPER	*(text)*
	Converts text to uppercase.
VALUE	*(text)*
	Converts a text argument to a number.

LOGICAL FUNCTIONS

AND	*(logical1,logical2,...)*
	Returns TRUE if all its arguments are TRUE.
FALSE	*()*
	Returns the logical value FALSE.
IF	*(logical_test,value_if_true,value_if_false)*
	Specifies a logical test to perform.
NOT	*(logical)*
	Reverses the logic of its argument.
OR	*(logical1,logical2,...)*
	Returns TRUE if any argument is TRUE.
TRUE	*()*
	Returns the logical value TRUE.

INFORMATION FUNCTIONS

CELL	*(info_type,reference)*
	Returns information about the formatting, location, or contents of a cell.
ERRORTYPE	*(value)*
	Returns a number corresponding to an error type.
INFO	*(type_text)*
	Returns information about the current operating environnement.
ISBLANK	*(value)*
	Returns TRUE if the value is blank.
ISERR	*(value)*
	Returns TRUE if the value is any error value except #N/A.
ISERROR	*(value)*
	Returns TRUE if the value is any error value.
ISLOGICAL	*(value)*
	Returns TRUE if the value is a logical value.
ISNA	*(value)*
	Returns TRUE if the value is the #N/A error value.
ISNONTEXT	*(value)*
	Returns TRUE if the value is not text.
ISNUMBER	*(value)*
	Returns TRUE if the value is a number.

Microsoft Excel 97

ISREF	*(value)*
	Returns TRUE if the value is a reference.
ISTEXT	*(value)*
	Returns TRUE if the value is text.
N	*(value)*
	Returns a value converted to a number.
NA	*()*
	Returns the error value #N/A.
TYPE	*(value)*
	Returns a number indicating the data type of a value.

!

A

AUTOCOMPLETE

C

CALCULATIONS

CELLS

CHARACTERS

CHARTS

COLUMNS/ROWS

COMMENTS

CONDITIONS

CONSOLIDATION

COPYING

CRITERIA

D

DATABASE

DATES

DELETING

DOCUMENTS

DRAWING OBJECTS

E

EDITING DATA

ENTERING DATA

F

FILTER

FINDING/REPLACING

FORMATTING

FORMULAS

Formula palette 28, 35
Names in formulas 27
Tracing cells used in formulas 12
see also CALCULATIONS,
FUNCTIONS, NAMES

FUNCTIONS

Inserting a function into a formula 35
List of integrated functions 92

H

HEADERS AND FOOTERS

Creating headers and footers 57

L

LINKS

Cancelling links between chart and
worksheet 74
Creating a link between worksheets 18
Hyperlink 17

M

MACROS

Creating, running 84
Opening an Add-In 84
Viewing macro contents 85

MARGINS

see PAGE SETUP, PRINT PREVIEW

MATRICES

See CALCULATIONS

MOVING

Going to a specific cell 10
Moving a sheet 18
Moving around in a sheet 9
Moving cell contents 24
Moving from one sheet to another 10

N

NAMES

Naming calculation formulas 26
Naming cells 26
Naming sheets 19
Replacing cell references with names 27
Using names in a formula 27

NUMBERS

see FORMATTING, ZERO

O

OUTLINES

Creating/destroying 52

P

PAGE SETUP

Gridlines 56
Margins 56
Orientation 45, 56
Page breaks 54
Scaling 56
Setting up a chart for printing 62

PIVOT TABLES

see TABLES

PRINTING

Charts 62
Print areas 53
Print preview 55
Print what ? 53
Reports 59
see also PAGE SETUP

PRINT PREVIEW

see PRINTING, PAGE SETUP

PROTECTION

Password to modify 15
Protecting documents 15
Protecting/unprotecting cells 42
Protecting/unprotecting sheets 19, 42

UNDOING/REPEATING

Actions   4 - 5

VIEWS/REPORTS

WORKBOOK

see also SHEETS, DOCUMENTS

ZERO

Displaying/hiding zero values   6

ZOOM

Zooming in on the workspace   6

INDEX BY SUBJECT